HLM:
Hierarchical Linear and Nonlinear Modeling with the HLM/2L and HLM/3L Programs

HLM™

Hierarchical Linear and Nonlinear Modeling
with the HLM/2L and HLM/3L Programs

Anthony S. Bryk
University of Chicago

Stephen W. Raudenbush
Michigan State University

Richard T. Congdon, Jr.
Harvard University

SSI SCIENTIFIC SOFTWARE INTERNATIONAL

Preface

New program features in HLM version 4

HLM version 4 offers a number of advances over version 3 in convenience of use. It greatly broadens the range of hierarchical models that can be estimated. Here is a guide to key new features and options:

1. **Windows interface**

   All models can be formulated in Windows. As you specify variables at each level, the relevant equations for each level are immediately constructed in a graphics box. These are saved and can be easily modified for subsequent analysis. Data are also easily read into HLM using Windows.

2. **Interface with widely available statistical packages**

   HLM version 4 can read data from a variety of statistical packages, including SPSS, SAS, SYSTAT, and STATA, to construct the SSM file. HLM version 4 outputs residual files that can immediately be read into these packages. Thus, all of the familiar exploratory analysis methods, data transformations, and graphical capabilities of these packages are readily available. See Chapter 2: *Working with HLM/2L*.

3. **Hierarchical Generalized Linear Models (Non-linear models)**

   HLM version 4 allows estimation of Bernoulli and binomial models for binary data with logit link function and Poisson models for count data with constant or variable exposure with log link function. Estimation is available for two- and three-level models with and without over-dispersion. Data may be at the person level or grouped by co-variate set. We refer to these as hierarchical generalized linear models (HGLM). (See Chapter 5: *Conceptual and Statistical Background for Hierarchical Generalized Linear Models (HGLM)* and Chapter 6 *Fitting HGLMs (Nonlinear Models)*.

4. Generalized Estimating Equations (GEE)

HGLM provides estimation of population-average models using Generalized Estimating Equations (GEE) with and without robust standard errors as described by Zeger, Liang, & Albert (1988).

5. Fisher Scoring/EM Algorithm

Earlier versions of HLM utilized an EM algorithm with an Aitken accelerator to maximize the likelihood. Version 4 offers acceleration via the Fisher scoring algorithm. The Fisher/EM combination produces a high standard of speed and reliable convergence for both two-level and three-level programs.

6. Standard Errors for Variance-Covariance Estimates

Full maximum likelihood for two- and three-level hierarchical linear models and full penalized quasi-likelihood (PQL; see Breslow & Clayton, 1993) estimates for hierarchical generalized linear models are accompanied by standard errors for variance-covariance components (see Chapter 2, including a cautionary note).

7. Plausible Value Analysis

Replicated analyses for multiply imputed data sets such as the National Assessment of Educational Progress, the National Adult Literacy Survey, and the International Adult Literacy Survey are now available for the two-level model. (See Chapter 7 *Plausible Value Averaging with HLM/2L.*)

8. Automated Production of Command Files

Interactive runs (either to create an SSM file or to execute an analysis) automatically output command files which can be executed via batch or read into Windows.

Contents

1 Conceptual and Statistical Background for Two-Level Models

Behavioral and social data commonly have a nested structure. For example, if repeated observations are collected on a set of individuals and the measurement occasions are not identical for all persons, the multiple observations are properly conceived as nested within persons. Each person might also be nested within some organizational unit such as a school or workplace. These organizational units may in turn be nested within a geographical location such as a community, state, or country. Within the hierarchical linear model, each of the levels in the data structure (*e.g.*, repeated observations within persons, persons within communities, communities within states) is formally represented by its own sub-model. Each sub-model represents the structural relations occurring at that level and the residual variability at that level.

This manual describes the use of the HLM computer programs for the statistical modeling of two- and three-level data structures, respectively. It should be used in conjunction with the text *Hierarchical Linear Models: Applications and Data Analysis Methods* (Bryk, A.S. & Raudenbush, S.W., 1992: Newbury Park, CA: Sage Publications). The HLM programs have been tailored so that the basic program structure, input specification, and output of results closely coordinate with this textbook. This manual also cross-references the appropriate sections of the textbook for the reader interested in a full discussion of the details of parameter estimation and hypothesis testing. Many of the illustrative examples described in this manual are based on data distributed with the program and analyzed in the Sage text.

We begin by discussing the two-level model below and the use of the HLM/2L program in Chapter 2. Building on this framework, Chapters 3 and 4 in-

1

troduce the three-level model and the use of the HLM/3L program. Chapters 5 and 6 introduce new material original to version 4 of HLM that detail use of hierarchical modeling for non-normal level-1 errors.

The general two-level model

As the name implies, a two-level model consists of two submodels at level 1 and level 2. For example, if the research problem consists of data on students nested within schools, the level-1 model would represent the relationships among the student-level variables and the level-2 model would capture the influence of school-level factors. Formally, there are $i = 1, \ldots, n_j$ level-1 units (*e.g.*, students) nested within $j = 1, \ldots, J$ level-2 units (*e.g.*, schools).

Level-1 model

We represent in the level-1 model the outcome for case i within unit j as:

$$
\begin{aligned}
Y_{ij} &= \beta_{0j} + \beta_{1j} X_{1ij} + \beta_{2j} X_{2ij} + \cdots + \beta_{Qj} X_{Qqj} + r_{ij} \\
&= \beta_{0j} + \sum_{q=1}^{Q} \beta_{qj} X_{qij} + r_{ij} ,
\end{aligned}
\tag{1.1}
$$

where

$\beta_{qj} (q = 0, 1, \ldots, Q)$ are *level-1 coefficients*;

X_{qij} is *level-1 predictor q* for case i in unit j;

r_{ij} is the *level-1 random effect*; and

σ^2 is the variance of r_{ij}, that is the *level-1 variance*.

Here we assume that the random term $r_{ij} \sim N(0, \sigma^2)$.

Level-2 model

Each of the level-1 coefficients, β_{qj}, defined in the level-1 model becomes an outcome variable in the level-2 model:

$$
\begin{aligned}
\beta_{qj} &= \gamma_{q0} + \gamma_{q1}W_{1j} + \gamma_{q2}W_{2j} + \cdots + \gamma_{qS_q}W_{S_qj} + u_{qj} \\
&= \gamma_{q0} + \sum_{s=1}^{S_q} \gamma_{qs}W_{sj} + u_{qj} \ ,
\end{aligned}
\tag{1.2}
$$

where

γ_{qs} $(q = 0, 1, \ldots, S_q)$ are *level-2 coefficients*;

W_{sj} is a *level-2 predictor*; and

u_{qj} is a *level-2 random effect*.

We assume that, for each unit j, the vector $(u_{0j}, u_{1j}, \ldots, u_{Qj})'$ is distributed as multivariate normal, with each element of u_{qj} having a mean of zero and variance of

$$
\mathsf{Var}(u_{qj}) = \tau_{qq} \ .
\tag{1.3}
$$

For any pair of random effects q and q',

$$
\mathsf{Cov}(u_{qj}, u_{q'j}) = \tau_{qq'} \ .
\tag{1.4}
$$

These *level-2 variance and covariance components* can be collected into a dispersion matrix, T, whose maximum dimension is $(Q + 1) \times (Q + 1)$.

We note that each level-1 coefficient can be modeled at level-2 as one of three general forms:

1. *a fixed level-1 coefficient; e.g.*,

$$
\beta_{qj} = \gamma_{q0} \ ,
\tag{1.5}
$$

2. *a non-randomly varying level-1 coefficient, e.g.,*

$$\beta_{qj} = \gamma_{q0} + \sum_{s=1}^{S_q} \gamma_{qs} W_{sj} , \qquad (1.6)$$

3. *a randomly varying level-1 coefficient, e.g.,*

$$\beta_{qj} = \gamma_{q0} + u_{qj} \qquad (1.7)$$

or

$$\beta_{qj} = \gamma_{q0} + \sum_{s=1}^{S_q} \gamma_{qs} W_{sj} + u_{qj} . \qquad (1.8)$$

The actual dimension of T in any application depends on the number of level-2 coefficients specified as randomly varying. We also note that a different set of level-2 predictors may be used in each of the $Q + 1$ equations that form the level-2 model.

Parameter estimation

Three kinds of parameters are estimated in a hierarchical linear model: empirical Bayes estimates of randomly varying level-1 coefficients; generalized least squares estimates of the level-2 coefficients; and maximum-likelihood estimates of the variance and covariance components.

Empirical Bayes ("EB") estimates of randomly varying level-1 coefficients, β_{qj}

These estimates of the level-1 coefficients for each unit j are optimal composites of an estimate based on the data from that unit and an estimate based on data from other similar units. Intuitively, we are borrowing strength from all of the information present in the ensemble of data to improve the level-1 coefficient estimates for each of the J units. These "EB" estimates are also referred to as "shrunken estimates" of the level-1 coefficients. They are produced by HLM as part of the residual file output (see page 11, *Model checking based on the residual file*). (For further discussion see *Hierarchical Linear Models*, pp. 39–44; 76–82.)

Generalized least squares (GLS) estimates of the level-2 coefficients, γ_{qs}

Substitution of the level-2 equations for β_{qj} into their corresponding level-1 term yields a single-equation linear model with a complex error structure. Proper estimation of the regression coefficients of this model (*i.e.*, the γ's) requires that we take into account the differential precision of the information provided by each of the J units. This is accomplished through generalized least squares. In the program output, the final generalized least squares estimates for the γ's are represented by Gqs. (For further discussion see *Hierarchical Linear Models*, pp. 32–39.)

Maximum likelihood estimates of variance and covariance components, σ^2 at Level 1, and T at Level 2

Because of the unbalanced nature of the data in most applications of hierarchical linear models (*i.e.*, n_j varies across the J units and the observed patterns on the level-1 predictors also vary), traditional methods for variance-covariance component estimation fail to yield efficient estimates. Through iterative computing techniques, such as the EM algorithm and Fisher scoring, maximum-likelihood estimates for σ^2 and T can be obtained. (For further discussion, see *Hierarchical Linear Models*, pp. 44–48; also Chapter 10). In the program output, these estimates are denoted by SIGMA-SQUARED and TAU respectively.

Some other useful statistics

Based on the various parameter estimates discussed above, HLM/2L and HLM/3L also compute a number of other useful statistics. These include:

1. *Reliability of $\hat{\beta}_{qj}$.*

    The program computes an overall or average reliability for each level-1 coefficient across the set of J level-2 units. These are denoted in the program output as RELIABILITY ESTIMATES and are calculated according to Equation 3.53 in *Hierarchical Linear Models*, p. 43.

2. *Least squares residuals* $(\hat{u}_{qj})$.

These residuals are based on the deviation of an ordinary least squares estimate of a level-1 coefficient, $\hat{\beta}_{qj}$, from its predicted or "fitted" value based on the level-2 model, *i.e.*,

$$\hat{u}_{qj} = \hat{\beta}_{qj} - \left(\hat{\gamma}_{q0} + \sum_{s=1}^{S_q} \hat{\gamma}_{qs} W_{sj}\right).$$

(1.9)

These least squares residuals are denoted in HLM residual files by the prefix OL before the corresponding variable names.

3. *Empirical Bayes residuals* (u_{qj}^*).

These residuals are based on the deviation of the empirical Bayes estimates, β_{qj}^*, of a randomly varying level-1 coefficient from its predicted or "fitted" value based on the level-2 model, *i.e.*,

$$u_{qj}^* = \beta_{qj}^* - \left(\hat{\gamma}_{q0} + \sum_{s=1}^{S_q} \hat{\gamma}_{qs} W_{sj}\right).$$

(1.10)

These are denoted in the HLM residual files by the prefix EB before the corresponding variable names. (For a further discussion and illustration of OL and EB residuals see *Hierarchical Linear Models*, pp. 41–42; and 76–80).

Hypothesis testing

Corresponding to the three basic types of parameters estimated in a hierarchical linear model (EB estimates of random level-1 coefficients, GLS estimates of the fixed level-2 coefficients, and the maximum-likelihood estimates of the variance and covariance components), are single-parameter and multi-parameter hypothesis-testing procedures. (See *Hierarchical Linear Models*, pp. 48–56). The current HLM programs execute a variety of hypothesis tests for the level-2 fixed effects and the variance-covariance components. These are summarized in Table 1.1.

Table 1.1

Hypothesis tests for the level-2 fixed effects and the variance-covariance components

Type of Hypothesis	Test Statistic	Program Output
Fixed level-2 effects		
Single Parameter: $H_0 : \gamma_{qs} = 0$ $H_1 : \gamma_{qs} \neq 0$	t-ratio[1]	Standard feature of the Fixed Effects Table for all level-2 coefficients.
Multiparameter: $H_0 : C'\gamma = 0$ $H_1 : C'\gamma \neq 0$	general linear hypothesis test (Wald test), chi-square test[2]	Optional output specification (see page 54).
Variance-covariance components		
Single-Parameter: $H_0 : \tau_{qq} = 0$ $H_1 : \tau_{qq} > 0$	Chi-square test[3]	Standard feature of the Variance Components Table for all level-2 random effects.
Multiparameter: $H_0 : \mathrm{T} = \mathrm{T}_0$ $H_1 : \mathrm{T} = \mathrm{T}_1$	Difference in deviances, likelihood ratio test.[4]	Optional output specification (see page 56).

[1] See Equation 3.65 in *Hierarchical Linear Models*.
[2] See Equation 3.73 in *Hierarchical Linear Models*.
[3] See Equation 3.82 in *Hierarchical Linear Models*.
[4] Here T_0 is a reduced form of T_1.

2 Working with HLM/2L

Data analysis by means of the HLM/2L program will typically involve three stages:

1. construction of the "SSM file" (the sufficient statistics matrices);
2. execution of analyses based on the SSM file; and
3. evaluation of fitted models based on a residual file.

We describe each stage below and illustrate each by means of an example using an interactive execution mode. We then consider batch execution. Finally, we illustrate a number of special options.

Constructing the SSM file from raw data

We assume that a user has employed a standard computing package to check and clean the data thoroughly, to recode or transform variables as needed, and to conduct relevant exploratory analyses, and that the user now wishes to fit a series of hierarchical linear models. The first task will be to construct the sufficient statistics file from raw data.

Two raw data files are required as input: a level-1 file and a level-2 file. The two files are linked by a common level-2 unit ID which must appear on every level-1 record that is linked to a particular level-2 unit. *Note, all level-1 cases must be grouped together by their respective level-2 unit ID.*

In the example below, the level-1 units are 7,185 students nested within 160 US High Schools as described in Chapter 4 of *Hierarchical Linear*

Models. In the first stage of the analysis, the HLM program will compute summary statistics based on the student data in the first school, merge this with the school-level data for that school, write a record in the SSM file that contains both the summarized student data and the school data, then repeat the process for the second school, and continue until all of the data are processed. The resulting file, called the SSM file, will have 160 records, that is, the number of level-2 units.

The SSM file is written in binary format for efficient storage and computation and therefore cannot be interpreted by the human eye. However, the user can execute the PRSSM2 sub-program in order to examine the contents of the SSM file. To execute this sub-program, simply type at the system prompt:

PRSSM2 *ssmfile*

(where *ssmfile* can be replaced by the SSM filename of the user's choice). This will translate the SSM file into ASCII format and store it in a file called *ssmfile*.OUT for subsequent review. To override the output filename, specify a filename as a second parameter on the command line, for example, OUTPUT:

PRSSM2 *ssmfile* OUTPUT

Handling of missing data

HLM/2L provides two options for handling missing data at level 1: pairwise deletion and listwise deletion of cases. These follow the conventional routines used in standard statistical packages for regression analysis and the general linear model. Although the pairwise option is included, we caution against its use, especially when the amount of missing data is substantial.

At level 2, HLM/2L assumes complete data. If you have missing data at level 2, you should either impute a value for the missing information or delete the units in question. *Prior to entering data into* HLM/2L *it is important to check that the level-2 file does not contain blanks or missing data codes as the program will read these as legitimate values.*

Executing analyses based on the SSM file

Once the SSM file is constructed, all subsequent analyses will be computed using the SSM file as input. It will therefore be unnecessary to read the larger student-level data file in computing these analyses. The efficient summary of data in the SSM file leads to faster computation. The SSM file is like a "system file" in a standard computing package in that it contains not only the summarized data but the names of all of the variables.

Model specification has three steps:

1. specifying the level-1 model, which defines a set of level-1 coefficients to be computed for each level-2 unit;
2. specifying a level-2 structural model to predict each of the level-1 coefficients; and
3. specifying the level-1 coefficients to be viewed as random.

The output produced from these analyses includes estimates, standard errors and approximate t-tests for the fixed coefficients defined in the level-2 model; estimates of variance and covariance components and approximate chi-square tests for the variance components; and a variety of auxiliary diagnostic statistics. Additional output options and hypothesis-testing procedures may be selected.

Model checking based on the residual file

After fitting a hierarchical model, it is wise to check the tenability of the assumptions underlying the model:

☐ Are the distributional assumptions realistic?

☐ Are results likely to be affected by outliers or influential observations?

☐ Have important variables been omitted or nonlinear relationships been ignored?

These questions and others can be addressed by means of analyses of the HLM residual file.

A residual file includes:

- ❑ Fitted values for each level-1 coefficient (that is, values predicted on the basis of the level-2 model)
- ❑ Ordinary least squares (OL) and empirical Bayes (EB) estimates of level-2 residuals (discrepancies between level-1 coefficients and fitted values)
- ❑ Dispersion estimates useful in exploring sources of variance heterogeneity at level 1
- ❑ Expected and observed Mahalanobis distance measures useful in assessing the multivariate normality assumption for the level-2 residuals
- ❑ Selected level-2 predictors useful in exploring possible relationships between such predictors and level-2 residuals

See Chapter 9 in *Hierarchical Linear Models* for a full discussion of these methods.

Windows, interactive, and batch execution

Formulation and testing of models using HLM programs can be achieved via Windows, interactive, or batch modes. Most PC users will find the Windows mode preferable. This draws on the visual features of Windows while preserving the speed of use associated with a command-oriented (batch) program. Non-PC users have the choice of interactive and batch modes only. Interactive execution guides the user through the steps of the analysis by posing questions and providing a menu of options. The interactive mode is especially helpful in familiarizing the user with the logic of the analytic method and the program. However, the batch mode can be considerably faster once the user becomes skilled in working with the program. In presenting the example below, we employ the interactive mode, turning our attention to batch execution in the section *Using* HLM/2L *in batch mode* on page 40. For guidance in the use of the Windows mode, see the help facility within the HLM/2L for Windows program.

An example using HLM/2L in interactive mode

Chapter 4 in *Hierarchical Linear Models* presents a series of analyses of data from the *High School and Beyond* survey. A level-1 model specifies the relationship between student socioeconomic status (*ses*) and mathematics achievement in each of 160 schools; at level-2, each school's intercept and slope are predicted by school sector (Catholic versus public) and school mean social class. We reproduce these analyses here (see Table 4.5 in *Hierarchical Linear Models*, p. 72).

Constructing the SSM file from raw data

PC users may construct the SSM file from a wide variety of input file types including SPSS, SAS, STATA, EXCEL, LOTUS and many others. TRANSYS, which is distributed with the HLM PC versions, must be installed. See the TRANSYS.DOC documentation file, distributed with the PC versions, for a full list of input file types supported.

Non-PC users may construct the SSM file with one of the following types of input files: ASCII data files, SYSTAT data files, or SAS V5 transport[1] files. We first illustrate the use of ASCII data files and then consider input from SYSTAT files and other statistical packages.

ASCII input

Data input requires a level-1 file (or student-level file) and a level-2 file (or school-level file).

---

[1]If the *SAS V5 transport* option is chosen and the SAS dataset (with the ssd extension) exists, but not the transport file (with the ssp extension), HLM/2L and HLM/3L will offer to create the transport file for you, but this will only work if you have SAS installed.

Level-1 file. For our example data, the level-1 file has 7185 cases and four variables (not including the *school id*). The variables are:

- ❑ *minority,* an indicator for student ethnicity (1 = minority, 0 = other)
- ❑ *female,* an indicator for student gender (1 = female, 0 = male)
- ❑ *ses,* (a standardized scale constructed from variables measuring parental education, occupation, and income)
- ❑ *mathach,* a measure of mathematics achievement

Data for the first ten and last ten cases are printed out below.

```
1224            0.000       0.000       0.022       4.583
1224            0.000       0.000       0.332      20.349
1224            0.000       0.000       0.372       6.714
1224            0.000       0.000      -0.078      16.405
1224            0.000       0.000      -0.158      17.898
1224            0.000       0.000      -0.298      19.338
1224            0.000       0.000      -0.458      21.521
1224            0.000       0.000      -0.468       3.154
1224            0.000       0.000      -0.468      21.178
1224            0.000       0.000      -0.528      20.349
 . . .
 . . .
 . . .
9586            0.000       1.000      -0.068       8.603
9586            0.000       1.000      -0.138      17.589
9586            0.000       1.000      -0.258      11.124
9586            0.000       1.000      -0.308      18.014
9586            0.000       1.000      -0.598       9.595
9586            0.000       1.000      -0.708      20.330
9586            0.000       1.000      -0.858       7.476
9586            1.000       1.000       0.542       9.071
9586            1.000       1.000       1.612      20.967
9586            1.000       1.000      -0.048      10.208
```

The first field in the data above is the level-2 unit id (in this case the *schoolid*). Thus, the first ten cases are students in school 1224; the last ten are in school 9586. The second variable is *minority,* which — for the first case — takes on a value of 0.000, indicating that that student is not a minority student. The next three variables are, respectively, *female, ses,* and *mathach.* The format of the data is (A4,8X,4F12.3). Notice that we have formatted the id code as A4, indicating it is alphanumeric and occupies the first four columns. *It is a convention in the* HLM/2L *program to format the level-2 unit id as an alphanumeric variable to distinguish it from the other variables.* Each of the numeric variables are formatted as F12.3, indicating that each occupies 12 columns and that there are three digits after the decimal point. The symbol 8X indicates that eight columns are to be skipped after the id field.

Note, all level-1 cases must be grouped together by their respective level-2 unit id. The easiest way to assure this is to sort the level-1 file by the level-2 unit id field prior to entering the data into HLM/2L.

Level-2 file. At level 2, the illustrative data set consists of 160 schools with 6 variables per school. The variables are:

❏ *size* (school enrollment)

❏ *sector* (1 = Catholic, 0 = public)

❏ *pracad* (proportion of students in the academic track)

❏ *disclim* (a scale measuring disciplinary climate)

❏ *himnty* (1 = more than 40% minority enrollment, 0 = less than 40%)

❏ *meanses* (mean of the SES values for the students in this school who are included in the level-1 file)

The data for the first and last ten schools are printed below:

1224	842.000	0.000	0.350	1.597	0.000	−0.428
1288	1855.000	0.000	0.270	0.174	0.000	0.128
1296	1719.000	0.000	0.320	−0.137	1.000	−0.420
1308	716.000	1.000	0.960	−0.622	0.000	0.534
1317	455.000	1.000	0.950	−1.694	1.000	0.351
1358	1430.000	0.000	0.250	1.535	0.000	−0.014
1374	2400.000	0.000	0.500	2.016	0.000	−0.007
1433	899.000	1.000	0.960	−0.321	0.000	0.718
1436	185.000	1.000	1.000	−1.141	0.000	0.569
1461	1672.000	0.000	0.780	2.096	0.000	0.683
.					
.					
.					
9198	833.000	1.000	0.970	−1.225	0.000	0.498
9225	1951.000	0.000	0.560	0.048	0.000	0.259
9292	2350.000	0.000	0.130	2.043	1.000	−0.588

9340	257.000	0.000	0.470	0.274	0.000	−0.391
9347	1067.000	1.000	0.580	−0.905	0.000	0.218
9359	1184.000	1.000	0.690	−0.475	0.000	0.360
9397	1314.000	0.000	0.440	−0.231	0.000	0.140
9508	1119.000	1.000	0.520	−1.138	0.000	−0.132
9550	1532.000	0.000	0.450	0.791	0.000	0.059
9586	262.000	1.000	1.000	−2.416	0.000	0.627

The first variable in the data above is again the level-2 id (here *schoolid*). Thus, the first case is 1224; the last case is school 9586. The second variable is *size*; note for example that school 1224 has a total enrollment of 842 students. The next five variables are, respectively, *sector, pracad, disclim, himnty*, and *meanses*. The format of the data is (A4,2X,6F12.3). Again, we have formatted the id code as A4. *For both the level-1 and the level-2 files, the level-2 id must be given the same alphanumeric format in both files*. Again, each of the numeric variables is formatted as F12.3, indicating that each occupies 12 columns and that there are three digits after the decimal point. The user may choose any format for the numeric variables.

While the input format statement for HLM resembles FORTRAN, only a subset of format options are acceptable. The user may specify:

1. The **A** format descriptor to read in the ID variable. This is followed by a number of columns that the id occupies.

2. The **F** format descriptor (and the E, used to read in numbers with exponents). This may be preceded with a number specifying a repeat value, and needs to be followed by a decimal number specifying both the number of columns that variable occupies and the places to the right of the decimal.

   For example, 4F12.3 tells HLM that there are four variables in a row occupying 12 columns and that each value has three numbers to the right of the decimal point.

3. The **X** format descriptor. This is used to skip over a number of columns. For example, 8X skips over eight columns when reading the data.

4. The **/** (forward slash) format descriptor. This tells HLM to go to the next line of the input file to read data. It is used when each case takes more than one line in the raw data file.

5. Commas have to be inserted to separate each of the descriptors.

6. Unlike FORTRAN, nesting of parentheses is not allowed (*e.g.*, (4A, 4(1X,F12.3))) will not be read properly by HLM programs).

Example: constructing an SSM file for the HS&B data. In the computer session that follows, all responses entered by the user are typed in a swiss font. All text presented in *italics* represents additional commentary we have added in this program guide to help the user understand what is happening in the program at that moment.

```
HLM2L                                    (type the program name at the system prompt to start)

            HLM/2L, release 4.01
            =====================

Data Input Phase:
_____

Will you be starting with raw data?  Y
Is the input file a v-known file?  N
Enter type of raw data:
    for ASCII input          enter 1
    for SYSTAT.SYS file       enter 2
    for SAS transport file    enter 3
    for other file types      enter 4
    Type?  1
```

The "for other file types" prompt is only present on DOS versions. If you have either TRANSYS or DBMS/COPY installed on your computer, you will be able to read data from virtually any file format as input to HLM.

```
Input number of level-1 variables (not including the character ID):  4
Input format of level-1 file (the first field must be the character ID)
   format:   (A4,8X,4F12.3)

Input name of level-1 file:  HSB1.DAT

Input number of level-2 variables (not including the character ID):  6
Input format of level-2 file (the first field must be the character ID)
   format:   (A4,2X,6F12.3)

Input name of level-2 file:  HSB2.DAT

  Enter 8 character name for level-1 variable number 1:  MINORITY
  Enter 8 character name for level-1 variable number 2:  FEMALE
  Enter 8 character name for level-1 variable number 3:  SES
  Enter 8 character name for level-1 variable number 4:  MATHACH
```

```
Enter 8 character name for level-2 variable number 1:  SIZE
Enter 8 character name for level-2 variable number 2:  SECTOR
Enter 8 character name for level-2 variable number 3:  PRACAD
Enter 8 character name for level-2 variable number 4:  DISCLIM
Enter 8 character name for level-2 variable number 5:  HIMINTY
Enter 8 character name for level-2 variable number 6:  MEANSES

Is there missing data in the level-1 file?  N
Is there a level-1 weighting variable?  N
Is there a level-2 weighting variable?  N

Enter name of SSM file:   HSB.SSM
```

HLM/2L will now proceed to create a sufficient statistics file. Note, had we indicated that missing data were present in the level-1 file, the following additional prompts would have come to the screen:

```
Is the missing value the same for all variables?  Y
Enter the number that represents missing data.  -99.0
Do you want pair-wise or list-wise deletion? (enter p or l)  L
```

Note that HLM/2L allows for the possibility of a different missing value code for each variable.

After computation of the SSM file, HLM/2L provides some basic descriptive statistics for all variables read at both level 1 and level 2. **It is important to review these results closely in order to assure that the data have been properly read into HLM/2L.** *Compare the results below, for example, with those in Hierarchical Linear Models, p. 61.*

LEVEL-1 DESCRIPTIVE STATISTICS

VARIABLE NAME	N	MEAN	SD	MINIMUM	MAXIMUM
MINORITY	7185	0.27	0.45	0.00	1.00
FEMALE	7185	0.53	0.50	0.00	1.00
SES	7185	0.00	0.78	-3.76	2.69
MATHACH	7185	12.75	6.88	-2.83	24.99

```
Do you wish to save these descriptive statistics in a file?  Y
```

LEVEL-2 DESCRIPTIVE STATISTICS

VARIABLE NAME	N	MEAN	SD	MINIMUM	MAXIMUM
SIZE	160	1097.82	629.51	100.00	2713.00
SECTOR	160	0.44	0.50	0.00	1.00

```
PRACAD          160      0.51      0.26      0.00      1.00
DISCLIM         160     -0.02      0.98     -2.42      2.76
HIMINTY         160      0.28      0.45      0.00      1.00
MEANSES         160     -0.00      0.41     -1.19      0.83
```

```
7185 level-1 records have been processed
 160 level-2 records have been processed
```

If you answer "Y" to the prompt about saving the descriptive statistics to a file, these two tables will be written to a file in your working directory. The file name will be HLM2SSM.STS. *In addition, whether you choose to save the descriptive statistics or not,* HLM/2L *will always write out a file named* CREATESS.RSP *which contains a log of the input responses given to create the SSM file. Should the SSM file appear incorrect for some reason, inspection of the log may provide a clue. Also, this file may be edited, renamed, and used as input to create a new SSM file. At the system prompt simply type, for example,*

```
    HLM2L -R CREATESS.NEW
```

where CREATESS.NEW *is the edited, renamed input file. The interactive prompts will be quickly sent to the screen and "answered" (by responses read from the file* CREATESS.NEW*), and the program will proceed automatically to recreate the SSM file.*

SYSTAT file input

Below is an example of an HLM/2L run to create a sufficient statistics file with input from SYSTAT system files:

HLM2L   *(issue the program name at the system prompt to start)*

```
                 HLM/2L, release 4.01
                 ====================
```

```
Data Input Phase:
_____
```

```
Will you be starting with raw data? Y
Is the input file a v-known file? N
Enter type of raw data:
   for ASCII input        enter 1
   for SYSTAT.SYS file    enter 2
```

```
        for SAS transport file    enter 3
        for other to file types   enter 4
        Type?  2

Input name of level-1 file?  STUDEG
Input name of level-2 file?  SCHEG
```

HLM/2L reads the following directly from the SYSTAT file:

```
The available level-1 variables are:
FOR      ID$  ENTER  1      FOR MINORITY  ENTER  2      FOR     FEMALE  ENTER  3
FOR      SES  ENTER  4      FOR  MATHACH  ENTER  5

What variable is the ID?  1

  Please specify level-1 variable # 1 (enter 0 to end):  2
  Please specify level-1 variable # 2 (enter 0 to end):  3
  Please specify level-1 variable # 3 (enter 0 to end):  4
  Please specify level-1 variable # 4 (enter 0 to end):  5
  Please specify level-1 variable # 5 (enter 0 to end):  0

The available level-2 variables are:
For      ID$ enter  1      For     SIZE enter  2      For   SECTOR enter  3
For   PRACAD enter  4      For  DISCLIM enter  5      For  HIMINTY enter  6
For   MEANSES enter  7

What variable is the ID?  1

  Please specify level-2 variable # 1 (enter 0 to end):  2
  Please specify level-2 variable # 2 (enter 0 to end):  3
  Please specify level-2 variable # 3 (enter 0 to end):  4
  Please specify level-2 variable # 4 (enter 0 to end):  5
  Please specify level-2 variable # 5 (enter 0 to end):  6
  Please specify level-2 variable # 6 (enter 0 to end):  7

Is there missing data in the level-1 file?  N

Is there a level-1 weighting variable?  N
Is there a level-2 weighting variable?  N

Enter name of SSM file:  SSMFILE
```

*Just as with ASCII file input, the program will now construct the sufficient
statistics matrices. Note, we did not have to type "0" to end the variable selection because HLM/2L recognized that all of the possible level-2 variables
had already been selected.*

SAS transport file input

The procedure for data input using SAS transport files is very similar to SYSTAT file input. Once the user has suggested the names for level-1 and level-2 SAS transport files, the variable lists are displayed from each file, and the user may choose the subset to be included in the SSM file construction. Options for handling missing data and design weights also appear.

Other formats for raw data

The PC implementation of HLM version 4 will read data from SPSS, STATA, EXCEL, LOTUS and many other formats as well as from SAS export, SYSTAT, and ASCII. The example below illustrates input from other packages, in this case from SPSS for Windows. The level-1 file is grpd.sav and the level-2 file is newsch.sav.

```
Will you be starting with raw data?   Y
Is the input file a v-known file?  N
Enter type of raw data:
     for ASCII input          enter 1
     for SYSTAT .SYS file      enter 2
     for SAS transport file    enter 3
     for other file types      enter 4
Type?  4

  Enter the appropriate TRANSYS keyword for your input file type
  (see the TRANSYS.DOC file for a list):  SPSSWIN
```

Note that in TRANSYS "SPSSWIN" is the designated keyword for system files created by SPSS for Windows.

```
When you are asked for an input filename, please enter it without
a suffix.

Input name of level-1 file:  GRPD

Converting file. Please wait a moment...

TRANSYS, The Tool For SYSTAT Formatted File Connectivity
Version=5.0
         Copyright 1989-94, Conceptual Software, Inc.
```

```
1277 Records Of 5 Variables and 46 Bytes Written To grpd.sys


Input name of level-2 file: NEWSCH

Converting file. Please wait a moment...

TRANSYS, The Tool For SYSTAT Formatted File Connectivity
Version=5.0
        Copyright 1989-94, Conceptual Software, Inc.

357 Records Of 2 Variables and 22 Bytes Written To newsch.sys
```

TRANSYS has just converted the SPSS system files into system files the HLM program can read. The prompts that appear next will display for the user the level-1 and level-2 variables available in the selected files. The user may then choose from these the variables to be included in the SSM file (as on page 20).

Executing analyses based on the SSM file

Once the SSM file is constructed, model fitting analyses are computed using the SSM file as input. As mentioned earlier, model specification via the interactive mode has three steps:

Step 1: Specification of the level-1 model. In our case we shall model mathematics achievement (*mathach*) as the outcome, to be predicted by student *ses*. Hence, the level-1 model will have two coefficients: the intercept and the *ses-mathach* slope.

Step 2: Specification of the level-2 prediction model. We shall predict each school's intercept by school *sector* and *meanses*. Similarly, each school's *ses-mathach* slope will be predicted by *sector* and *meanses*.

Step 3: Specification of level-1 coefficients as random or non-random. We shall model both the intercept and the slope as having randomly varying residuals. That is, we are assuming that the intercept and slope vary not only as a function of the two predictors, *sector* and *meanses*, but also as a function of a unique school effect. The two school residuals (*e.g.*, for the intercept and slope) are assumed sampled from a bivariate normal distribution.

The interactive program mode also poses a number of questions about output options and additional procedures. We comment on these as they arise in the computing session reproduced below.

Here is an example of an HLM/2L session in the interactive mode. At the system command line prompt, we first type the program name — HLM2L — followed by the name of the sufficient statistics file — HSB.SSM. The program now takes the user directly into the model specification process.

```
HLM2L HSB.SSM

                    SPECIFYING A LEVEL-1 OUTCOME VARIABLE

Please specify a level-1 outcome variable
 The choices are:
 For MINORITY enter  1  For    FEMALE enter  2    For    SES enter  3
 For  MATHACH enter  4

What is the outcome variable:  4

Do you wish to:

    Examine means,variances,chi-squared, etc? Enter 1
    Specify an HLM model?                      Enter 2
    Define a new outcome variable?             Enter 3
    Exit?                                      Enter 4

What do you want to do?  2
```

Option 1 is detailed in the section "Preliminary exploratory analysis with HLM/2L" on page 51.

```
                    SPECIFYING AN HLM MODEL

Level-1 predictor variable specification

Which level-1 predictors do you wish to use?
 The choices are:
 For MINORITY enter  1   For    FEMALE enter  2   For    SES enter  3

 level-1 predictor? (Enter 0 to end)  3
 level-1 predictor? (Enter 0 to end)  0

 Do you want to center any level-1 predictors?  Y
 (Enter 0 for no centering, enter 1 for group-mean, 2 for grand-mean)
 How do you want to center     SES?  1
```

Note, we have selected group-mean centering for the level-1 predictor, SES.

```
Do you want to set the level-1 intercept to zero in this analysis?  N
```

An answer of "Y" here specifies a level-1 model without an intercept or constant term.

```
Level-2 predictor variable specification

Which level-2 variables do you wish to use?

The choices are:
For      SIZE enter  1    For    SECTOR enter  2    For    PRACAD enter  3
For   DISCLIM enter  4    For   HIMINTY enter  5    For   MEANSES enter  6

Which level-2 predictor to model INTRCPT    ?
Level-2 predictor? (Enter 0 to end)  2
Level-2 predictor? (Enter 0 to end)  6
Level-2 predictor? (Enter 0 to end)  0

Which level-2 predictor to model  SES slope  ?
Level-2 predictor? (Enter 0 to end)  2
Level-2 predictor? (Enter 0 to end)  6
Level-2 predictor? (Enter 0 to end)  0

Do you want to constrain the variances in any of the level-2 random
  effect to zero?  N
```

An answer of "Y" here causes HLM/2L to list out the level-l coefficients and asks the user whether the corresponding random effect should be set to zero. An answer of "Y" to one of these probes is equivalent to specifying that level-1 coefficient as a fixed (or non-randomly varying) effect.

```
Do you want to center any level-2 predictors?  N
```

Note, the user has the option of selecting grand-mean centering for each of the level-2 predictors.

```
                          ADDITIONAL PROGRAM FEATURES

Select the level-2 variables that you might consider for
inclusion as predictors in subsequent models.
The choices are:
For      SIZE enter  1    For    SECTOR enter  2    For    PRACAD enter  3
For   DISCLIM enter  4    For   HIMINTY enter  5    For   MEANSES enter  6
```

```
Which level-2 variables to model INTRCPT1?
 Level-2 variable? (Enter 0 to end)  1
 Level-2 variable? (Enter 0 to end)  3
 Level-2 variable? (Enter 0 to end)  4
 Level-2 variable? (Enter 0 to end)  5
 Level-2 variable? (Enter 0 to end)  0
Which level-2 variables to model     SES slope?
 Level-2 variable? (Enter 0 to end)  -1
```

For all of the level-2 predictors selected here, HLM/2L will compute approximate "t-to-enter statistics" which can be used to guide specification of subsequent HLM/2L models. Note, the code "-1" tells HLM/2L to use for the SES slope model the same set of level-2 predictors as selected for the previous level-2 equation (i.e., the model for INTRCPT1).

OUTPUT SPECIFICATION

```
How many iterations do you want to do?  100
 Enter a problem title:  Intercept and Slopes-as-Outcomes Model
 Enter name of output file:  HSB1.LIS
Computing . . ., please wait
Starting values computed.  Iterations begun.
```

While the program is running, HLM/2L sends to the screen the value of the likelihood function computed for each iteration. We have printed below just the first and last three. Because the change between the 30th and 31st iterations was very small, the program automatically terminated before the requested 100 iterations were computed. The sensitivity of this "automatic stopping value" can be controlled by the user (see section "Table of keywords and options" on page 42).

Produced along with the output file is a file called "newcmd.hlm" which is a command file constructed by HLM based on the interactive session just completed. This file may be renamed and modified with an ASCII editor (for example, EDIT under DOS) for a subsequent batch-mode application. (See page 31 and following.)

```
The value of the likelihood function at iteration 1 = -2.325843E+004
The value of the likelihood function at iteration 2 = -2.325825E+004
The value of the likelihood function at iteration 3 = -2.325817E+004
 .
 .
 .
```

```
The value of the likelihood function at iteration 59 = -2.325737E+004
The value of the likelihood function at iteration 60 = -2.325737E+004
The value of the likelihood function at iteration 61 = -2.325737E+004
```

*Note: If you wish to terminate the computations early, press the Ctrl–C key combination **once**. This will stop the analysis after the current iteration and provide a full presentation of results based on that iteration.*

If you press Ctrl–C more than once, however, computation is terminated immediately and all output is lost.

Annotated HLM/2L output

Here is the output produced by the interactive session described above.

```
****************************************************************
*                                                              *
*      H   H  L      M      M   22                             *
*      H   H  L      MM    MM  2  2                            *
*      HHHHH  L      M M  M M     2      Version 4.01          *
*      H   H  L      M      M     2                            *
*      H   H  LLLLL  M      M   2222                           *
*                                                              *
****************************************************************
```

```
SPECIFICATIONS FOR THIS HLM RUN                 Thu Feb  8 17:43:13 1996
------------------------------------------------------------------------
  Problem Title: Intercept and Slopes-as-Outcomes Model

  The data source for this run = HSB.SSM                Name of the SSM file
  Output file name             = HSB1.LIS               Name of this output file
  The maximum number of level-2 units = 160             There are 160 schools
  The maximum number of iterations = 100
  Method of estimation: restricted maximum likelihood

Weighting Specification
-----------------------
                          Weight
                          Variable
            Weighting?    Name        Normalized?
  Level 1      no                         no
  Level 2      no                         no

  The outcome variable is  MATHACH
```

The model specified for the fixed effects was:
```
-------------------------------------------------------
Level-1                  Level-2
Coefficients             Predictors
--------------------     ---------------
        INTRCPT1, B0     INTRCPT2, G00
                          SECTOR, G01
                          MEANSES, G02
*       SES slope, B1    INTRCPT2, G10
                          SECTOR, G11
                          MEANSES, G12
```

'*' - This level-1 predictor has been centered around its group mean.

The model specified for the covariance components was:
```
-------------------------------------------------------
        Sigma-squared (constant across level-2 units)

        Tau dimensions
            INTRCPT1
                 SES slope
```

Summary of the model specified (in equation format)
```
-------------------------------------------------
```

Level-1 Model

$$Y = B0 + B1*(SES) + R$$

Level-2 Model

$$B0 = G00 + G01*(SECTOR) + G02*(MEANSES) + U0$$
$$B1 = G10 + G11*(SECTOR) + G12*(MEANSES) + U1$$

The information presented on the first page or two of the HLM/2L printout summarizes key details about the SSM file (e.g., number of level-2 units, whether weighting was specified), and about both the fixed and random effects models specified for this run. In this particular case, we are estimating the model specified by Equations 4.11 and 4.15 in Hierarchical Linear Models.

Level-1 OLS regressions
```
----------------------
```

Level-2 Unit	INTRCPT1	SES slope
1224	9.71545	2.50858
1288	13.51080	3.25545
1296	7.63596	1.07596
1308	16.25550	0.12602

```
1317          13.17769        1.27391
1358          11.20623        5.06801
1374           9.72846        3.85432
1433          19.71914        1.85429
1436          18.11161        1.60056
1461          16.84264        6.26650
```

As a program default, HLM/2L prints out the ordinary least squares (OL) regression equations, based on the level-1 model, for the first 10 units. When first analyzing a new data set, examining the OL equations for all of the units may be helpful in identifying possible outlying cases and bad data. The section "Table of keywords and options" on page 42 describes how to use the LEV1OLS command to change the number of units printed out here.

```
The average OLS level-1 coefficient for INTRCPT1 =      12.62075
The average OLS level-1 coefficient for      SES =       2.20164
```

This is a simple average of the OL coefficients across all units which had sufficient data to permit a separate OL estimation.

```
STARTING VALUES
---------------

sigma(0)_squared =      36.72025

  Tau(0)
  INTRCPT1      2.56964        0.28026
       SES      0.28026       -0.01614

  New Tau(0)
  INTRCPT1      2.56964        0.28026
       SES      0.28026        0.43223


The outcome variable is  MATHACH

Estimation of fixed effects
(Based on starting values of covariance components)
-----------------------------------------------------------------------
   Fixed Effect     Coefficient   Standard Error  T-ratio   P-value
-----------------------------------------------------------------------
For           INTRCPT1, B0
   INTRCPT2, G00    12.095864       0.204343       59.194    0.000
     SECTOR, G01     1.226266       0.315204        3.890    0.000
    MEANSES, G02     5.335184       0.379879       14.044    0.000
```

```
For           SES slope, B1
   INTRCPT2, G10      2.935410        0.168691       17.401     0.000
     SECTOR, G11     -1.634083        0.260672       -6.269     0.000
    MEANSES, G12      1.015061        0.323523        3.138     0.002

The value of the likelihood function at iteration 1 = -2.325843E+004
The value of the likelihood function at iteration 2 = -2.325825E+004
The value of the likelihood function at iteration 3 = -2.325817E+004
The value of the likelihood function at iteration 4 = -2.325812E+004
The value of the likelihood function at iteration 5 = -2.325798E+004
  .
  .
  .
The value of the likelihood function at iteration 57 = -2.325737E+004
The value of the likelihood function at iteration 58 = -2.325737E+004
The value of the likelihood function at iteration 59 = -2.325737E+004
The value of the likelihood function at iteration 60 = -2.325737E+004

Iterations stopped due to small change in likelihood function
```

Below are the estimates of the variance and covariance components from the final iteration and selected other statistics based on them.

```
******* ITERATION 61 *******

  Sigma—squared =      36.70313                          Level-1 variance component

  Tau
  INTRCPT1      2.37996      0.19058                      Level-2 variance-covariance
       SES      0.19058      0.14892                                      components

  Tau (as correlations)
  INTRCPT1  1.000  0.320                                 Level-2 variance-covariance
       SES  0.320  1.000                                   components expressed
                                                                   as correlations

  ---------------------------------------------------
   Random level-1 coefficient   Reliability estimate
  ---------------------------------------------------
                                                          These are average reliability
   INTRCPT1, B0                       0.733             estimates for the random level-1
        SES, B1                       0.073                             coefficients.

The value of the likelihood function at iteration 61 = -2.325737E+004
```

The next two tables present the final estimates for the fixed effects and variance components and related test statistics. These results are slightly more precise than those reported in Table 4.5, p. 72 of Hierarchical Linear Models, because they are based on the more efficient computing routines used in versions 3 and higher.

The outcome variable is MATHACH

Final estimation of fixed effects:

Fixed Effect	Coefficient	Standard Error	T-ratio	P-value
For INTRCPT1, B0				
INTRCPT2, G00	12.096006	0.198734	60.865	0.000
SECTOR, G01	1.226384	0.306272	4.004	0.000
MEANSES, G02	5.333056	0.369161	14.446	0.000
For SES slope, B1				
INTRCPT2, G10	2.937981	0.157135	18.697	0.000
SECTOR, G11	-1.640954	0.242905	-6.756	0.000
MEANSES, G12	1.034427	0.302566	3.419	0.001

Final estimation of variance components:

Random Effect	Standard Deviation	Variance Component	df	Chi-square	P-value
INTRCPT1, U0	1.54271	2.37996	157	605.29503	0.000
SES slope, U1	0.38590	0.14892	157	162.30867	0.369
level-1, R	6.05831	36.70313			

Statistics for current covariance components model

Deviance = 46514.74077
Number of estimated parameters = 4

Exploratory Analysis: estimated level-2 coefficients and their standard
       errors obtained by regressing EB residuals on level-2 predictors
       selected for possible inclusion in subsequent HLM runs

----

Level-1 Coefficient		Potential Level-2 Predictors		

	SIZE	PRACAD	DISCLIM	HIMINTY
INTRCPT1,B0				
Coefficient	0.000	0.690	-0.161	-0.543
Standard Error	0.000	0.404	0.106	0.229
t value	1.569	1.707	-1.516	-2.372

	SIZE	PRACAD	DISCLIM	HIMINTY
SES,B1				
Coefficient	0.000	0.039	-0.005	-0.058
Standard Error	0.000	0.044	0.012	0.025
t value	1.297	0.899	-0.425	-2.339

The results of this exploratory analysis suggest that HIMINTY might be a good candidate to include in the INTRCPT1 model. The t-values represent the approximate result that will be obtained when one additional predic-

tor is added to any of the level-2 equations. This means that if HIMINTY is added to the model for the INTRCPT1, for example, the apparent relationship suggested above for HIMINTY in the SES slope model might disappear. (For a further discussion of the use of these statistics see discussion in Hierarchical Linear Models, p. 214 on "Approximate t-to-Enter Statistics.")

The HLM/2L command file

As detailed in the section *Using HLM/2L in batch mode* on page 40, the user can control which questions come to the screen by means of a "command file." At one extreme, the command file is virtually empty and questions regarding every possible optional procedure or output will come to the screen. At the other extreme, the command file specifies the answer to every question that might arise, in which case the analysis is performed completely in batch mode. In between the two extremes are a large number of possibilities in which various questions are answered in the command file while other questions come to the screen. Hence, the execution can be partly batch and partly interactive.

The command file presented below also estimates the Intercept and Slopes-as-Outcomes Model for the HS&B data. The italicized comments provide a brief description of each command function. A more complete discussion of each of the keywords and related options in this command file appears in the section *Table of keywords and options* on page 42.

```
level1:mathach=intrcpt1+ses,1+random                    Specifies the level-1 model.
level2:intrcpt1=intrcpt2+sector+meanses+random/size,pracad,disclim,himinty
level2:ses=intrcpt2+sector+meanses+random/size,pracad,disclim,himinty
                        Specifies the level-2 model and other level-2 predictors for possible
                        inclusion in subsequent models for both intrcpt1 and the ses slope.
numit:100                         Sets the maximum number of iterations.
lev1ols:10              Controls the number of level-1 OLS regressions printed out.
resfil:n                          Controls whether a residual file is created.
hypoth:n                 Disables some optional hypothesis testing procedures.
stopval:.000001          Sets the criteria for automatically stopping the iterations.
constrain:n             Estimates a model with constrained level-2 coefficients.
fixtau:3                 Alternative options for generating starting values.
output:hsb1.lis                  File where HLM/2L output will be saved.
title:Intercept and Slopes-as-Outcome Model               Title on page 1 of output.
nonlin:n                          Switch to do a nonlinear analysis.
```

See Chapter 5 and 6 for details on the last entry (nonlinear analysis).

Model checking based on the residual file

The residual file produced by HLM/2L provides the data analyst with a means of checking the fit and distributional assumptions of the model. This file will contain the EB residuals (see Equation 1.10 above), OL residuals (see Equation 1.9 above), and fitted values (i.e., $\hat{\gamma}_{q0} + \Sigma\hat{\gamma}_{qs}W_{sj}$) for each level-1 coefficient. By adding the OL residuals to the corresponding fitted values, the analyst can also obtain the OL estimate $\hat{\beta}_{qj}$ of the corresponding level-1 coefficient, β_{qj}. Similarly, by adding the EB residuals to the fitted values, we obtain the EB estimate β^*_{qj} of the level-1 coefficient, β_{qj}.

In addition, the file will contain Mahalanobis distances (which are discussed below), estimates of the total and residual standard deviations (log metric) within each unit, the values of the predictors used in the level-2 model, and any other level-2 prediction variables selected by the user.

The interactive prompts to specify a residual file are illustrated below. Note that the user will *not* be prompted by HLM/2L for a residual file specification when the line resfil:n is present in the default command file, COMFILE2.HLM. For more details see p. 41.

```
                        OUTPUT SPECIFICATION

Do you want a residual file? Y

Enter type of stat package you will use:
    for SYSTAT   enter 1
    for SAS      enter 2
    for SPSS     enter 3
    Type?    1

Select additional variables to go in residual file.
  The choices are:
  For      SIZE enter  1    For    SECTOR enter  2    For    PRACAD enter   3
  For   DISCLIM enter  4    For   HIMINTY enter  5    For   MEANSES enter   6

  Level-2 variable (Enter 0 to end)  1
  Level-2 variable (Enter 0 to end)  3
  Level-2 variable (Enter 0 to end)  5
  Level-2 variable (Enter 0 to end)  0
```

These prompts will continue until all of the variables have been chosen or 0 is entered. All level-2 predictors used in the analysis in addition to the variables selected above will be included in the residual file.

In batch mode, adding the following lines to your command file will also accomplish the task:

```
refil:y/size,pracad,himinty
resfiltype:SPSS
```

Below is an example of a SYSTAT version of a residual file.

```
SAVE RESFIL
LRECL=255
INPUT (ID$,NJ,CHIPCT,MDIST,LNTOTVAR,OLSRSVAR,MDRSVAR,
EBINTRCP,EBSES     ,
OLINTRCP,OLSES     ,
FVINTRCP,FVSES     ,
    SIZE,
  SECTOR,   PRACAD,  HIMINTY,  MEANSES,
),($12,#5,5*#11,/ 2*#11/ 2*#11/ 2*#11,/ 5*#12)
if CHIPCT=-99 then let CHIPCT=.
if MDIST=-99 then let MDIST=.
if LNTOTVAR=-99 then let LNTOTVAR=.
if OLSRSVAR=-99 then let OLSRSVAR=.
if MDRSVAR=-99 then let MDRSVAR=.
if OLINTRCP=-99 then let OLINTRCP=.
if OLSES   =-99 then let OLSES   =.
RUN
```

HLM/2L specifies missing values as "-99" in the residual file. This series of if statements recodes these values to the SYSTAT missing value code of "."

```
      1224       47     0.0187     0.0033     2.0274     2.0164     2.0054
     -0.0734    -0.0047
     -0.0980     0.0133
      9.8135     2.4952
    842.00000    0.00000    0.35000    0.00000   -0.42800
      1288       25     0.1187     0.1475     1.9494     1.9202     1.8991
      0.4559     0.0421
      0.7322     0.1851
     12.7786     3.0704
   1855.00000    0.00000    0.27000    0.00000    0.12800
      1296       48     2.7386     2.4598     1.6777     1.6799     1.6841
     -1.7102    -0.2234
     -2.2202    -1.4276
      9.8561     2.5035
   1719.00000    0.00000    0.32000    1.00000   -0.42000
```

(Only the data from the first three units are reproduced here.)

Once a residual file has been created, it is necessary to read it into SAS, SPSS, SYSTAT, or another statistical package in order to construct various diagnostic plots. The first several lines of the residual file (see the example above) are commands that can be used to read the residual file into SYSTAT. If your installation has SYSTAT, simply issue the following commands:

If your installation does not have SAS, SPSS, or SYSTAT, the commands in the residual file provide you with file layout information that will be needed in order to create, for example, a BMDP input statement.

Structure of the residual file

The first part of the SYSTAT "INPUT" statement contains variable names, and the second part contains information pertaining to variable type (a dollar sign for character variables and a pound sign for numeric variables) and variable length. The slashes in the second part of the input statement mark the start of a new record or line in the data file. A residual file will generally contain five records per unit. The first record has one 12-byte character field (unit *ID*), one 5-byte numeric field, (*NJ*), and five 11-byte numeric fields (for *CHIPCT* through *MDRSVAR*). (The first record will have the same format in all applications). The second record contains in this case two 11-byte numeric fields for the two EB residuals; the third record contains two 11-byte numeric fields for the OL residuals; and the fourth record also contains two 11-byte numeric fields for the fitted or predicted values of the level-1 coefficients based on the estimated level-2 models. The last record contains the level-2 predictors used in the analysis plus those additional level-2 predictors requested by the user for inclusion in the file. In this case it consists of five 12-byte numeric fields.

While most of this is straightforward, the information contained in the first record for each unit merits elaboration. *NJ* is the number of cases for level-2 unit j. It is followed by two variables, *CHIPCT* and *MDIST*. If we are modeling q level-1 coefficients, then *MDIST* would be the Mahalanobis distance (*i.e.*, the standardized squared distance of a unit from the center of a v-dimensional distribution, where v is the number of random effects per unit. Essentially, *MDIST* provides a single, summary measure of the distance of a unit's EB estimates, β^*_{qj} from its "fitted value," $\hat{\gamma}_{q0} + \Sigma \hat{\gamma}_{qs} W_{sj}$. Note that the units in the residual file are sorted in ascending order by *MDIST*. If the normality assumption is true, then the Mahalanobis distances should be distributed approximately $\chi^2(v)$. Analogous to univariate normal probability plotting, we can construct a Q-Q plot of

MDIST vs. *CHIPCT*. *CHIPCT* are the expected values of the order statistics for a sample of size J selected from a population that is distributed $\chi^2(v)$. If the **Q-Q** plot resembles a 45 degree line, we have evidence that the random effects are distributed v-variate normal. In addition, the plot will help us detect outlying units (*i.e.*, units with large *MDIST* values well above the 45 degree line). It should be noted that such plots are good diagnostic tools only when the level-1 sample sizes, *NJ*, are at least moderately large. (For further discussion see *Hierarchical Linear Models*, p. 218.)

After *MDIST*, record 1 contains three estimates of the level-1 variability: the natural logarithm of the total standard deviation within each unit, *LNTOTVAR*; the natural logarithm of the residual standard deviation within each unit based on its least squares regression, *OLSRSVAR* (note, this estimate exists only for those units which have sufficient data to compute level-1 OL estimates); and the *MDRSVAR*, the natural logarithm of the residual standard deviation from the final fitted fixed effects model. The natural log of these three standard deviations with the addition of a bias-correction factor for varying degrees of freedom is reported (see *Hierarchical Linear Models*, p. 169). We note that these statistics can be used as input for the V-known program in research on group-level correlates of diversity (Raudenbush & Bryk, 1987).

Some possible residual analyses

We illustrate below some of the possible uses of a residual file in examining the adequacy of fitted models and in considering other possible level-2 predictor variables. (For a full discussion of this topic see Chapter 9 of *Hierarchical Linear Models*.)

Here are the basic statistics for each of the variables created as part of the HLM/2L residual file.

```
TOTAL OBSERVATIONS:    160

                        NJ    CHIPCT    MDIST   LNTOTVAR   OLSRSVAR
       N OF CASES      160       160      160        160        160
       MINIMUM      14.000     0.006    0.003      1.265      1.272
       MAXIMUM      67.000    11.537   13.251      2.138      2.088
       MEAN         44.906     1.991    2.010      1.821      1.790
       STANDARD DEV 11.855     1.967    2.146      0.150      0.137
```

	MDRSVAR	EBINTRCP	EBSES	OLINTRCP	OLSES
N OF CASES	160	160	160	160	160
MINIMUM	1.272	-3.719	-0.406	-7.714	-3.558
MAXIMUM	2.088	4.164	0.474	5.545	3.803
MEAN	1.790	0.000	-0.000	-0.011	-0.018
STANDARD DEV	0.137	1.313	0.154	1.847	1.461

	FVINTRCP	FVSES	SIZE	SECTOR	PRACAD
N OF CASES	160	160	160	160	160
MINIMUM	5.760	0.517	100.000	0.000	0.000
MAXIMUM	17.754	3.647	2713.000	1.000	1.000
MEAN	12.632	2.220	1097.825	0.438	0.514
STANDARD DEV	2.491	0.775	629.506	0.498	0.256

	HIMINTY	MEANSES
N OF CASES	160	160
MINIMUM	0.000	-1.188
MAXIMUM	1.000	0.831
MEAN	0.275	-0.000
STANDARD DEV	0.448	0.414

Examining heterogeneity of level-1 variance.   Below is a stem-and-leaf plot of the residual dispersions for the 160 schools based on the final fitted model. This can be helpful in suggesting possible causes of heterogeneity of level-1 variances. (See the section *Testing homogeneity of level-1 variances* on page 55 for how to test this hypothesis within HLM/2L.) We see from the information below that there are three schools where the within-school standard deviation, σ_j, is considerably smaller than we would expect under a homogeneity hypothesis. (For a further discussion see *Hierarchical Linear Models*, pp. 207–210.)

```
          STEM AND LEAF PLOT OF VARIABLE:  MDRSVAR    , N =    160

MINIMUM IS:      1.281
LOWER HINGE IS:      1.715
MEDIAN IS:       1.830
UPPER HINGE IS:      1.893
MAXIMUM IS:      2.106
```

```
       12   8
       13   4
       14   3
***OUTSIDE VALUES***
       14   6
       15   0122
       15   568
       16   12233344
       16   556677788899
       17 H 0000001111112223333334444
       17   5567778888899
       18 M 0000112222233334444444444
       18 H 5555556666666666777788889999
       19   000011222223333444
       19   667777788899
       20   012334
       20
       21   0
```

Examining OL and EB residuals.   Figure 2.1 shows a plot of the OL vs. EB residuals for the SES slopes. As expected the EB residuals for the SES slope are much more compact than the OL residuals. While the latter range between $(-4.0, 4.0)$, the range for the EB residuals is only $(-0.5, 0.5)$. (For a further discussion see *Hierarchical Linear Models*, pp. 76–82.)

Next, in Figure 2.2, we see a plot of the OL vs. EB residuals for the intercepts. Notice that while the EB intercepts are "shrunk" as compared to the OL estimates, the amount of shrinkage for the intercepts is far less than for the SES slopes above.

Exploring the potential of other possible level-2 predictors.   Figure 2.3 shows a plot of EB residuals against a possible additional level-2 predictor, *PRA-CAD*, for the intercept model. Although the relationship appears slight (a correlation of 0.15), *PRACAD* will enter this model as a significant predictor. (For a further discussion of the use of residual plots in identifying possible level-2 predictors see *Hierarchical Linear Models*, pp. 212–214.)

Examining possible nonlinearity of a level-2 predictor's relationship to an outcome.   Next, in Figure 2.4, is an example of a plot of EB residuals, in this case for the *SES* slope, against a variable included in the model. This plot suggests that the assumption of a linear relationship between the *SES* slope

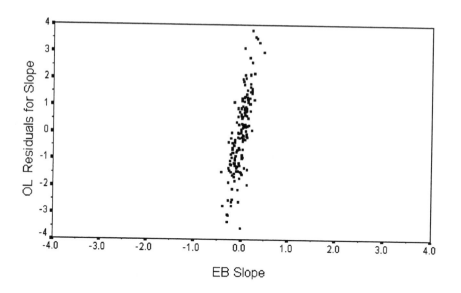

Figure 2.1

OL versus EB residuals for the SES slopes

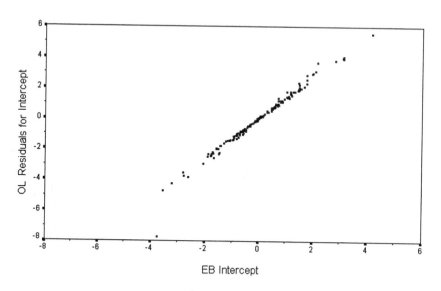

Figure 2.2

OL versus EB residuals for the intercepts

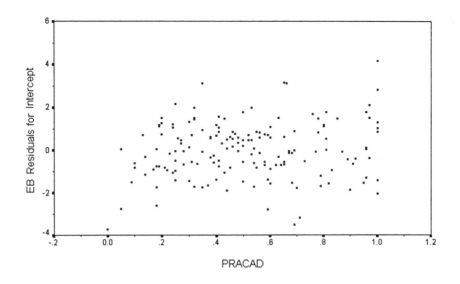

Figure 2.3

EB residuals against a possible additional level-2 predictor, PRACAD, for the intercept model

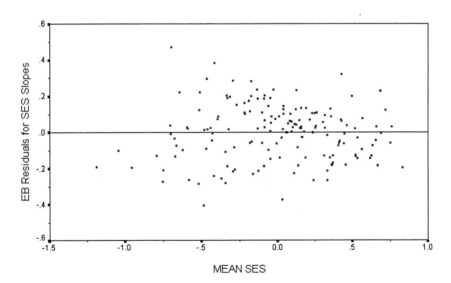

Figure 2.4

EB residuals for SES slope against MEANSES

and *MEANSES* is appropriate. (That is, the residuals appear randomly distributed around the zero line without regard to values of *MEANSES*.)

Using HLM/2L in batch mode

Overview

As mentioned above, the non-Windows user may choose a fully interactive execution mode, a fully batch execution mode, or an execution mode that is partly interactive and partly batch:

❑ *Fully interactive mode*

No specifications are made in the command file. Hence, the program will prompt the user with questions concerning every program feature.

❑ *Fully batch mode*

The run is fully specified in the command file. No questions come to the screen.

❑ *Partly interactive, partly batch mode*

Some specification occurs in the command file; the program prompts the user with questions for the remaining program features.

Perhaps the rarest execution mode in practice will be the fully interactive mode. The reason is that many specialized features of the program will be of interest only occasionally, so that it will be convenient to "turn these questions off" by answering them in the command file.

Command file keywords

A command file consists of a series of lines. Each line begins with a keyword followed by a colon, after the colon is the option chosen by the user, *i.e.*,

```
keyword:option
```

For example, HLM/2L provides several optional hypothesis-testing procedures, described in detail in the section *Other program features* on page 51. Suppose the user does not wish to use these optional procedures in a given analysis. Then the following line would be included in the command file:

hypoth:n

The keyword hypoth concerns the optional hypothesis testing procedures; the option chosen ('n') indicates that the user does not wish to employ these procedures. Alternatively, the user might include the line:

hypoth:y

This causes HLM/2L to send the optional hypothesis testing menu to the screen during model specification in the interactive mode. Lines beginning with a '#' sign are ignored and may be used to put comments in the command file.

Table of keywords and options

Table 2.1 presents the list of keywords and options recognized by HLM/2L. Examples with detailed explanation follow.

The default command file

A basic command file called COMFILE2.HLM is used by HLM/2L as a default unless the user specifies an alternative command file (see below). This file is kept in a system-dependent location. Under DOS, it is usually in the C:\HLM directory.

The italicized comments provide a brief description of each command function. A more complete discussion of each of the keywords and related options in this command file appears in *Table of keywords and options* on page 42.

levlols:10   *Ten level-1 OLS coefficients will be printed.*
fixtau:3   *Use the "standard" computer-generated starting values for the variances and covariances.*
constrain:n   *The user is not interested in constraining any of the level-2 coefficients.*

Table 2.1

Keywords and options for the HLM/2L command file

Keyword	Function	Option	Definition
level1	Level-1 model specification	intrcpt1 *varname* *varname*,1 *varname*,2	Level-1 intercept Level-1 predictor (no centering) Level-1 predictor centered around group (or level-2 unit) mean Level-1 predictor centered around grand mean
	(Note: variable names may be specified in either upper or lower case.)		
level2	Level-2 model specification	intrcpt2 *varname* *varname*,2 /*varlist*	Level-2 intercept Level-2 predictor (no centering) Level-2 predictor centered around grand mean List after the slash level-2 variables for exploratory analysis and "t-to-enter" statistics.
numit	Maximum number of iterations	*positive integer*	
accel	Controls iteration acceleration	*integer* ≥ 3	Selects how often the accelerator is used. Default is 5.
lev1ols	Number of units for which OL equations should be printed	*positive integer*	Default is 10.
constrain	Constraining of gammas	n y	No constraining Yes: two or more gammas will be constrained. (The program will prompt the user interactively to set the constraints. Alternatively, constraints can be set in the command file; see *Constraints on the fixed effects*, p. 62).
hypoth	Select optional hypothesis testing menu	y n	Yes: sends optional hypothesis testing menu to the screen during interactive mode use. No. (Note, during batch execution, hypoth:n should be selected in order to suppress screen prompt. Select desired options through keywords below.)

Continues

2 WORKING WITH HLM/2L

Table 2.1 (continued)

Keywords and options for the HLM/2L command file

Keyword	Function	Option	Definition
gamma#	Specifies a particular multivariate contrast to be tested	*(see example on page 55)*	In any single run, HLM/2L will test up to 5 multivariate hypotheses. Each hypothesis may consist of up to 5 contrasts. Each contrast is specified by its own line in the command file. The contrast associated with the first hypothesis is specified with the keyword gamma1. For the second hypothesis, the keyword is gamma2 and for the third it is gamma3. (See section *Multivariate hypothesis tests for fixed effects*, p. 54 for further discussion and illustration.)
homvar	Test homogeneity of level-1 variance	y n	Yes No
deviance	Deviance statistic from prior analysis	*positive real number*	
df	Degrees of freedom associated with deviance statistic from prior analysis (use only if "deviance" has been specified)	*positive integer*	
fixtau	Method of correcting unacceptable starting values	1 2 3 4 5	Set all off-diagonal elements to 0 Manually reset starting values Automatic fix-up (default) Terminate run Stop program even if starting values are acceptable; display starting values and then allow user to manually reset them.
fixsigma2	Controls σ^2	n *real number* > 0	Default: does not restrict σ^2. Fixes σ^2 to the specified value.
stopval	Convergence criterion for maximum likelihood estimation	*positive real number*	Example: .000001. Can be specified to be more (or less) restrictive.
mlf	Controls maximum likelihood estimation method	n y	Default (restricted maximum likelihood) Full maximum likelihood. Produces standard errors of T and σ^2.

Continues

Table 2.1 (continued)

Keywords and options for the HLM/2L command file

Keyword	Function	Option	Definition
resfil	Create a residual file	y n */varlist*	Yes No List after the slash additional level-2 variables to be included in the residual file.
resfilname	Name of residual file	*filename*	Changes the default. Defaults are: resfil.cmd for SYSTAT, resfil.sys for SPSS, and resfil.sas for SAS.
resfiltype	Type for residual file	SYSTAT SAS SPSS	Selects program type to be used in subsequent analysis of residual file.
title			Program label up to 64 characters
output	Filename of file that contains output	*filename*	Will be written to disk; output will overwrite a file of same name.

The following keywords are specific to nonlinear analysis

Keyword	Function	Option	Definition
nonlin	Selects a nonlinear analysis	bernoulli poisson binomial,*countvar* poisson,*countvar*	These options are explained in detail in Chapter 6.
macroit	Maximum number of macro iterations	*positive integer*	
microit	Maximum number of micro iterations	*positive integer*	
stopmacro	Convergence criterion for change in parameters across macro iterations	*positive integer*	
stopmicro	Convergence criterion for micro iterations	*positive real number*	Note: same function as stopval in a linear analysis.
plausvals	Selects a list of plausible values for multiple imputation application	*varlist*	See Chapter 7.

Execution of a command file

The execution of a command file is accomplished by typing the following command at the system prompt:

HLM2L *ssmfile comfile*

The command HLM2L tells the computer to execute the HLM2L.EXE program which resides in your path. The first parameter, *ssmfile*, indicates that a file by this name contains the sufficient statistics for the analysis; and the second parameter, *comfile*, indicates the command file to be used in the analysis. We have reproduced below the command file to execute the intercept and slopes-as-outcomes model in batch mode.

```
level1:mathach=intrcpt1+ses,1+random
level2:intrcpt1=intrcpt2+sector+meanses+random/size,pracad,disclim,himinty
level2:ses=intrcpt2+sector+meanses+random/size,pracad,disclim,himinty
numit:100
lev1ols:10
resfil:n
hypoth:n
stopval:.000001
constrain:n
fixtau:3
output:out01
title:Intercept and Slopes-as-Outcome Model
nonlin:n
```

We now take a closer look at this command file to see exactly how the computer interprets each command.

1. `level1:mathach=intrcpt1+ses,1+random`

   The level-1 model specifies *mathach* as an outcome to be predicted by the level-1 intercept plus student *ses*. The ",1" in ses,1 indicates that *ses* will be centered around its school mean. (Alternatively, ses,2 would stipulate centering around the grand mean.) This statement corresponds to the equation

   $$Y_{ij} = \beta_{0j} + \beta_{1j}(X_{ij} - \bar{X}_{\cdot j}) + r_{ij} \, ,$$

   where

Y_{ij} is the *mathach* score for student i in school j,

β_{0j} is the intercept for school j,

X_{ij} is the *ses* value for student i in school j,

$\bar{X}_{.j}$ is the mean *ses* for school j,

β_{1j} is the regression slope associated with *ses* for school j, and

r_{ij} is a random error.

On the cover page of the HLM/2L output, this equation is represented as:

```
Y=B0+B1*(SES)+R
```

The cover page will also note any centering options selected for level-1 or level-2 predictors.

2. Following the command line for the level-1 model is the level-2 model for the level-1 intercept, β_{0j}:

```
level2:intrcpt1=intrcpt2+sector+meanses
        +random/size,pracad,disclim,himinty
```

Thus, at level 2, the level-1 intercept is viewed as depending on a level-2 intercept plus the effect of *sector* plus the effect of *meanses* plus a random school effect. To gauge the likely importance of *size*, *pracad*, *disclim*, and *himinty* as predictors in a subsequent model, empirical Bayes residuals from the analysis will be regressed on each of these potential predictors; the effects, their estimated standard errors, and approximate "t-to-enter" statistics will be printed.

The model for the level-1 intercept is

$$\beta_{0j} = \gamma_{00} + \gamma_{01}(sector)_j + \gamma_{02}(meanses)_j + u_{0j} ,$$

where

γ_{00} is the expected intercept for a school with values of zero on the predictors *sector* and *meanses*,

γ_{01} and γ_{02} are regression coefficients associated with *sector* and *meanses*, respectively, and

u_{0j} is the unique random effect associated with school j.

On the cover page of the HLM/2L output, this equation will be represented as:

```
B0=G00+G01*(SECTOR)+G02*(MEANSES)+U0
```

3. Similarly, the command line to model the level-1 slope, β_{1j}, is:

```
level2:ses=intrcpt2+sector+meanses
           +random/size,pracad,disclim,himinty
```

Here, the *ses-mathach* slope for each school is also viewed as depending on a level-2 intercept, the effects of *sector* and *meanses*, and a random school effect. The same set of level-2 predictors will be assessed for possible inclusion in subsequent models of the *ses-mathach* slope.

The current model for the *ses-mathach* slope is

$$\beta_{1j} = \gamma_{10} + \gamma_{11}(\textit{sector})_j + \gamma_{12}(\textit{meanses})_j + u_{1j} \,,$$

where

γ_{10} is the expected slope for a school with values of zero on the predictors *sector* and *meanses*,

γ_{11} and γ_{12} are regression coefficients associated with *sector* and *meanses*, respectively, and

u_{1j} is the unique random effect associated with school j.

The representation in the HLM/2L output for this equation is:

```
B1=G10+G11*(SECTOR)+G12*(MEANSES)+U1
```

4. `numit:100`

The maximum number of iterations is 100. If the program fails to converge by the 100th iteration, computation will terminate and results associated with the 100th iteration will be printed.

5. `lev1ols:10`

The ordinary least squares estimates for the first 10 level-2 units will be printed. Note that there are 160 schools in the illustrative data set. The user could set `lev1ols` to any positive integer up to 160 in this example (*i.e.*, the maximum value of $j = J$).

6. `constrain:n`

   None of the fixed effects (the gammas) will be constrained to be equal to other gammas.

7. `resfil:n`

   No residual file will be output.

8. `hypoth:n`

   No optional hypothesis tests will be utilized.

9. `fixtau:3`

   If the initial estimate of the variance-covariance matrix at level-2 is not positive definite, option 3, an "automatic fix-up," will be invoked.

10. `title:Intercept and Slopes-as-Outcomes Model`

    The title listed above will appear on the first page of the output.

11. `output:out01`

    The listing file from the analysis will be written to a file named out01 in your working directory.

12. `nonlin:n`

    This will not be a nonlinear analysis.

Some examples of model specification via a command file

To illustrate some of the modeling capacities of HLM/2L via a command file we present below the specification that will reproduce the results of the five basic models presented in Chapter 4 of *Hierarchical Linear Models* for analyzing the HS&B data. (Only the command lines for `level1` and `level2` are presented.)

1. Oneway ANOVA with Random Effects

Model:

$$Y_{ij} = \beta_{0j} + r_{ij}$$
$$\beta_{0j} = \gamma_{00} + u_{0j}$$

Command file:

```
level1:mathach=intrcpt1+random
level2:intrcpt1=intrcpt2+random
```

Representation in the output file:

```
Y=B0+R
B0=G00+U0
```

2. Regression with Means as Outcomes

Model:

$$Y_{ij} = \beta_{0j} + r_{ij}$$
$$\beta_{0j} = \gamma_{00} + \gamma_{01}(\text{mean ses})_j + u_{0j}$$

Command file:

```
level1:mathach=intrcpt1+random
level2:intrcpt1=intrcpt2+meanses+random
```

Representation in the output file:

```
Y=B0+R
B0=G00+G01*(MEANSES)+U0
```

3. Random Coefficient Model

Model:

$$Y_{ij} = \beta_{0j} + \beta_{1j}(X_{ij} - \bar{X}_{\cdot j}) + r_{ij}$$
$$\beta_{0j} = \gamma_{00} + u_{0j}$$
$$\beta_{1j} = \gamma_{10} + u_{1j}$$

Command file:

```
level1:mathach=intrcpt1+ses,1+random
level2:intrcpt1=intrcpt2+random
level2:ses=intrcpt2+random
```

Representation in the output file:

```
Y=B0+B1*(SES)+R
B0=G00+U0
B1=G10+U1
```

4. *Intercepts and Slopes-as-Outcomes Model*

Model:

$$Y_{ij} = \beta_{0j} + \beta_{1j}(X_{ij} - \bar{X}_{\cdot j}) + r_{ij}$$
$$\beta_{0j} = \gamma_{00} + \gamma_{01}(\text{mean ses})_j + \gamma_{02}(\text{sector})_j + u_{0j}$$
$$\beta_{1j} = \gamma_{10} + \gamma_{11}(\text{mean ses})_j + \gamma_{12}(\text{sector})_j + u_{1j}$$

Command file:

```
level1:mathach=intrcpt1+ses,1+random
level2:intrcpt1=intrcpt2+meanses+sector+random
level2:ses=intrcpt2+meanses+sector+random
```

Representation in the output file:

```
Y=B0+B1*(SES)+R
B0=G00+G01*(MEANSES)+G02*(SECTOR)+U0
B1=G10+G11*(MEANSES)+G12*(SECTOR)+U1
```

Other program features

Preliminary exploratory analysis with HLM/2L

The first option in the basic HLM/2L menu "Examine means, variances, chi-squared, etc.?" provides a variety of statistics useful as we begin to formulate HLM/2L problems. The use of this option and a description of the output appears below.

```
HLM2L HSB.SSM

              SPECIFYING A LEVEL-1 OUTCOME VARIABLE

Please specify a level-1 outcome variable
 The choices are:
 For MINORITY enter  1    For   FEMALE enter  2    For     SES enter  3
 For  MATHACH enter  4

What is the outcome variable: 4

Do you wish to:
   Examine means,variances,chi-squared, etc? Enter 1
   Specify an HLM model?                      Enter 2
   Define a new outcome variable?             Enter 3
   Exit?                                      Enter 4

What do you want to do?  1
```

Below is the output that HLM/2L sends to the screen.

```
The outcome variable is  MATHACH
```

potential level-1 predictors	mean univariate regression coefficient	ANOVA estimate of variance in regression coefficient	reliability	chi-squared	j
MEANS	12.74785	8.76642	0.90192	1618.70998	160
MINORITY	-2.72109	5.60227	0.30517	228.41290	136
FEMALE	-0.94302	0.27533	0.05944	143.41090	123
SES	2.10355	0.46634	0.17531	212.38315	160

```
0 level-2 units were deleted because of no variance in  MATHACH
```

The display above presents information from a series of univariate regressions conducted separately on each unit. The outcome variable selected

*for these regressions is displayed at the top (MATHACH). The row enti-
tled "MEANS" provides the statistics from a one-way ANOVA on the outcome variable in the 160 schools. The remaining lines summarize the result from the respective univariate regressions estimated separately in each
school. The mean univariate coefficient averaged across the J schools is
reported in the first column. Column 2 provides an ANOVA-type estimate
of the parameter variability in these univariate coefficients. The average
reliability and chi-squared test statistics for homogeneity among the univariate regressions are reported in the third and fourth columns.*

*These data provide our first information about which level-1 coefficients
might be specified as random. Though very preliminary results, they suggest that both minority and ses coefficients might be specified as random.
Note, these are just univariate regression coefficients and are not adjusted
for any other level-1 effect as they would be in a full level-1 model.*

```
Hit return to continue < HRt>

Do you wish to:

    Examine correlations among univariate
    coefficients and level-2 variables?      Enter 1
    Specify an HLM model?                     Enter 2
    Define a new outcome variable?            Enter 3
    Exit?                                     Enter 4

What do you want to do?  1
```

*At this point, the user identifies which of the univariate regression coeffi-
cients computed above are to be considered further. In this instance we will
chose all three. (The unit mean is automatically included.)*

```
Please enter the level-1 univariate slopes you wish to estimate

The choices are:
For MINORITY enter  1    For   FEMALE enter  2    For     SES enter  3

level-1 predictor? (Enter 0 to end)  1
level-1 predictor? (Enter 0 to end)  2
level-1 predictor? (Enter 0 to end)  3
```

*Next, we select the level-2 predictors which might be used to model the
means and univariate regression slopes.*

```
Please enter the level-2 predictors you wish to estimate

The choices are:
For     SIZE enter  1    For   SECTOR enter  2    For    PRACAD enter  3
For  DISCLIM enter  4    For  HIMINTY enter  5    For   MEANSES enter  6

level-2 predictor? (Enter 0 to end)  1
level-2 predictor? (Enter 0 to end)  2
level-2 predictor? (Enter 0 to end)  3
level-2 predictor? (Enter 0 to end)  4
level-2 predictor? (Enter 0 to end)  5
level-2 predictor? (Enter 0 to end)  6


The correlation matrix among level-1 univariate coefficients
(Diagonal elements are standard deviations)


Predictors     MEANS    MINORITY    FEMALE      SES

    MEANS      3.1177
 MINORITY      0.1238    4.2846
   FEMALE     -0.0639    0.0978     2.1522
      SES      0.0135   -0.5121    -0.2078    1.6310

Hit return to continue < HRt>
```

These are simple correlations and standard deviations among the univariate regression coefficients estimated in the 160 schools.

```
The correlation matrix among level-2 predictors
(Diagonal elements are standard deviations)


Predictors      SIZE     SECTOR    PRACAD    DISCLIM   HIMINTY   MEANSES

    SIZE     629.5064
  SECTOR     -0.4519    0.4976
  PRACAD     -0.3150    0.6724    0.2559
 DISCLIM      0.3554   -0.7125   -0.6119    0.9770
 HIMINTY      0.1150    0.0494   -0.0792    0.0373    0.4479
 MEANSES     -0.1296    0.3553    0.6491   -0.3493   -0.4056    0.4140

Hit return to continue < HRt>
```

These are simple correlations among the level-2 predictors.

```
Correlations between level-2 predictors and level-1 univariate coefficients


Level-2        Level-1 univariate coefficients
Predictors      MEANS    MINORITY    FEMALE      SES

       SIZE    -0.0982    -0.1862    -0.2591    0.2008
     SECTOR     0.4492     0.3680     0.1199   -0.3977
     PRACAD     0.6821     0.2152     0.0612   -0.2017
    DISCLIM    -0.4678    -0.4343    -0.1038    0.3355
    HIMINTY    -0.3752     0.0790    -0.0004   -0.1964
    MEANSES     0.7847     0.0626     0.0576    0.0496


Hit return to continue < HRt>
```

The display above contains our first cross-level information. It presents information on the level-2 predictors that might be associated with the unit means and univariate regression coefficients. It suggests a list of candidate variables which might be included in the level-2 model for each level-1 coefficient. Again, this too is preliminary because the level-2 coefficients used here are univariate. Nonetheless they are informative.

```
Do you wish to:

    Specify an HLM model?                    Enter 1
    Define a new outcome variable?           Enter 2
    Exit?                                    Enter 3

What do you want to do?  3
```

Multivariate hypothesis tests for fixed effects

If you wish to pose a multivariate hypothesis test among the fixed effects, including hypoth: y in the command file will cause HLM/2L to prompt during interactive use for the specification of the contrasts to be tested. Below is an example using the Intercepts and Slopes-as-Outcomes Model.

```
Do you wish to use any of the optional hypothesis testing procedures?  Y
Do you wish to specify a multivariate hypothesis for the fixed effects?  Y
Enter contrast value for  INTRCPT1/INTRCPT2 (0 to ignore)  0
Enter contrast value for            /  SECTOR (0 to ignore)  1
Enter contrast value for            / MEANSES (0 to ignore)  0
Enter contrast value for        SES/INTRCPT2 (0 to ignore)  0
Enter contrast value for            /  SECTOR (0 to ignore)  0
Enter contrast value for            / MEANSES (0 to ignore)  0
```

```
Do you wish to specify another contrast as part of this hypothesis?  Y
  Enter contrast value for INTRCPT1/INTRCPT2 (0 to ignore)  0
  Enter contrast value for          /  SECTOR (0 to ignore)  0
  Enter contrast value for          / MEANSES (0 to ignore)  0
  Enter contrast value for      SES/INTRCPT2 (0 to ignore)  0
  Enter contrast value for          /  SECTOR (0 to ignore)  1
  Enter contrast value for          / MEANSES (0 to ignore)  0

Do you wish to specify another contrast as part of this hypothesis?  N

Do you wish to specify another hypothesis?  N
```

Alternatively, this contrast can also be specified in the command file by adding the following lines:

> gamma1:0.0,1.0,0.0,0.0,0.0,0.0

> gamma1:0.0,0.0,0.0,0.0,1.0,0.0

These commands test a composite null hypothesis:

$$H_0 : \gamma_{01} = \gamma_{11} = 0$$

where γ_{01} is the effect of sector on the intercept and γ_{11} is the effect of sector on the *ses* slope. The HLM/2L output associated with this test appears in the section *Selected HLM/2L output to illustrate optional hypothesis testing procedures* on page 57. (For a further discussion of this multivariate hypothesis test for fixed effects see *Hierarchical Linear Models*, pp. 50–52; 74–75).

Testing homogeneity of level-1 variances

HLM/2L assumes homogeneity of residual variance at level 1. That is, it specifies a common σ^2 within each of the J level-2 units. As an option, HLM/2L will test the adequacy of this assumption. Assuming hypoth:y appears in the command file, the following prompt will appear during interactive execution:

```
Do you wish to test the homogeneity of the level-1 variance?  Y
```

Alternatively, under batch execution the user should add to the command file:

```
homvar:y
```

The HLM/2L output associated with this test also appears in the section *Selected HLM/2L output to illustrate optional hypothesis testing procedures* on page 57. (For a further discussion of this test see *Hierarchical Linear Models*, pp. 207–211. We advise that users review these pages carefully before using this procedure.)

Multivariate tests of variance-covariance components specification

As noted in the section *Hypothesis testing* on page 6, HLM/2L also provides, as an option, a multiparameter test for the variance-covariance components. This likelihood-ratio test compares the deviance statistics of a restricted model with a more general alternative. The user must input the value of the deviance statistic and related degrees of freedom for the alternative specification. Again, assuming that hypoth:y is specified in the command file, the following prompts will appear during interactive execution:

```
Do you wish to test the specification for the variance-covariance components
against an alternative model?
(Note: the same fixed effects,must be specified in both models)  Y

Enter the deviance statistic value  46512.978
Enter the number of variance-covariance parameters  4
```

This test can also be requested under batch execution by adding the commands

```
deviance:46512.978

df:4
```

The HLM/2L output associated with this test appears in the section below. (For a further discussion of this multiparameter test see *Hierarchical Linear Models*, pp. 55–56; 75–76).

Selected HLM/2L output to illustrate optional hypothesis testing procedures

```
***************************************************************
*                                                             *
*      H    H   L       M    M   22                           *
*      H    H   L       MM  MM   2  2                         *
*      HHHHH    L       M  M  M     2      Version 4.01       *
*      H    H   L       M    M      2                         *
*      H    H   LLLLL   M    M   2222                         *
*                                                             *
***************************************************************
```

SPECIFICATIONS FOR THIS HLM RUN   Thu Feb 8 17:44:31 1996

   Problem Title: test options

   The data source for this run = hsb.ssm
   Output file name   = hsb3.lis
   The maximum number of level-2 units = 160
   The maximum number of iterations = 100
   Method of estimation: restricted maximum likelihood
Weighting Specification

```
                        Weight
                        Variable
            Weighting?  Name       Normalized?
Level 1     no                     no
Level 2     no                     no
```

   The outcome variable is MATHACH

   The model specified for the fixed effects was:

```
   Level-1                Level-2
   Coefficients           Predictors
   --------------------   ---------------
        INTRCPT1, B0        INTRCPT2, G00
                              SECTOR, G01
                              MEANSES, G02
#*      SES slope, B1       INTRCPT2, G10
                              SECTOR, G11
                              MEANSES, G12
```

'#' - The residual parameter variance for this level-1 coefficient has been set
     to zero.
'*' - This level-1 predictor has been centered around its group mean.

   The model specified for the covariance components was:

```
        Sigma-squared (constant across level-2 units)
        Tau dimensions
               INTRCPT1
```

```
Summary of the model specified (in equation format)
----------------------------------------------------
Level-1 Model

    Y = B0 + B1*(SES) + R

Level-2 Model

    B0 = G00 + G01*(SECTOR) + G02*(MEANSES) + U0
    B1 = G10 + G11*(SECTOR) + G12*(MEANSES)
```

Note, the middle section of output has been deleted. We proceed directly to the final results page.

```
The outcome variable is  MATHACH

Final estimations of fixed effects:
------------------------------------------------------------------------
    Fixed Effect      Coefficient   Standard Error  T-ratio   P-value
------------------------------------------------------------------------
For        INTRCPT1, B0
    INTRCPT2, G00     12.096251       0.198643        60.894     0.000
      SECTOR, G01      1.224401       0.306117         4.000     0.000
     MEANSES, G02      5.336698       0.368978        14.463     0.000
For       SES slope, B1
    INTRCPT2, G10      2.935860       0.150705        19.481     0.000
      SECTOR, G11     -1.642102       0.233097        -7.045     0.000
     MEANSES, G12      1.044120       0.291042         3.588     0.001

Final estimation of variance components:

------------------------------------------------------------------------
Random Effect          Standard      Variance     df   Chi-square  P-value
                       Deviation     Component
------------------------------------------------------------------------
INTRCPT1,    U0         1.54118        2.37523     157   604.29893   0.000
 level-1,    R          6.06351       36.76611

Statistics for current covariance components model
--------------------------------------------------
Deviance =  46515.81787
Number of estimated parameters =    2
```

For the likelihood ratio test, the deviance statistic reported above is compared with the value from the alternative model input by the user. The result of this test appears below.

```
Variance-Covariance components test
-----------------------------------
Chi-square statistic        =      2.84131
Number of degrees of freedom =   2
P-value                     = 0.240
```

A model which constrains the residual variance for the SES slopes, B1, to zero appears appropriate. (For a further discussion of this application see Hierarchical Linear Models, pp. 75–76. Note, the statistics reported here differ slightly from those in the text because of the improved computing routines in versions 3 and higher of HLM/2L.)

```
Test of homogeneity of level-1 variance
---------------------------------------
Chi-square statistic        =    244.08641
Number of degrees of freedom =  159
P-value                     = 0.000
```

These results indicate that there is variability among the J (= 160) level-2 units in terms of the residual within-school (i.e., level-1) variance. (For a full discussion of these results see Hierarchical Linear Models, pp. 207–211.)

```
                  Results of General Linear Hypothesis Testing
-----------------------------------------------------------------------
                                 Coefficients      Contrast
-----------------------------------------------------------------------
For       INTRCPT1, B0
     INTRCPT2, G00                12.096251     0.000   0.000
       SECTOR, G01                 1.224401     1.000   0.000
       MEANSES, G02                5.336698     0.000   0.000
For       SES slope, B1
     INTRCPT2, G10                 2.935860     0.000   0.000
       SECTOR, G11                -1.642102     0.000   1.000
       MEANSES, G12                1.044120     0.000   0.000

Chi-square statistic = 65.626400
Degrees of freedom   = 2
P-value              = 0.000000
```

The table above reminds the user of the multivariate contrast specified. The chi-square statistic and associated p-value indicate that it is highly unlikely that the observed estimates for G01 and G11 could have occurred under the specified null hypothesis.

Models without a level-1 intercept

In some circumstances, researchers may wish to estimate models without a level-1 intercept. Consider, for example, a hypothetical study in which three alternative treatments are implemented within each of J hospitals. One might estimate the following level-1 (within-hospital) model:

$$Y_{ij} = \beta_{1j} X_{1ij} + \beta_{2j} X_{2ij} + \beta_{3j} X_{3ij} + r_{ij} ,$$

where X_{qij} ($q = 1, 2, 3$) are indicator variables taking on a value of 1 if patient i in hospital j has received treatment q, 0 otherwise; and β_{qj} is the mean outcome in hospital j of those receiving treatment q. At level-2, the treatment means β_{qj} are predicted by characteristics of the hospitals. Of course, the same data could alternatively be modeled by a level-1 intercept and two treatment contrasts per hospital, but researchers will sometimes find the no-intercept approach convenient.

To see how this type of model is implemented using the command file, let us suppose that the variable names *treat1*, *treat2*, and *treat3* represent the dummy variables indicating whether a subject received treatment one, treatment two, or treatment three, respectively. The level-2 predictor, *public*, indicates whether a hospital is public (as opposed to private). We shall model each treatment mean as depending on the public versus private status of the hospital. Also, we wish to estimate the residual variance in these means over hospitals. To implement the no-intercept model, the researcher types the following lines in the command file:

```
level1:outcome=treat1+treat2+treat3+random

level2:treat1=intrcpt2+public+random

level2:treat2=intrcpt2+public+random

level2:treat3=intrcpt2+public+random
```

Alternatively, the same model may be estimated interactively by answering "Y" to the question "Do you want to set the level-1 intercept to zero in this analysis?" Note, this prompt can be suppressed during interactive use of the program by inserting the following line in the command file:

```
nobase:n
```

An example of a no-intercept model appears on page 144 of *Hierarchical Linear Models*. The vocabulary growth of young children is of interest. Both common sense and the data indicated that children could be expected to have no vocabulary at 12 months of age. Hence, the level-1 model contained no intercept:

$$Y_{ti} = \pi_{1i}(age_{ti} - 12) + \pi_{2i}(age_{ti} - 12)^2 + e_{ti} \,,$$

where age_{ti} is the age of child i at time t in months and Y_{ti} is the size of that child's vocabulary at that time. The corresponding line in the command file would look as follows:

```
level1:vocab=age12+age12sq+random
```

where   age12 $= age_{ti} - 12$ and   age12sq $= (age_{ti} - 12)^2$.

Notice that the word intrcpt1 is absent from this line of the command file.

Coefficients having a random effect with no corresponding fixed effect

A researcher may find it useful at times to model a level-1 predictor as having a random effect but no fixed effect. For example, it might be that gender differences in educational achievement are, on average, null across a set of schools; yet, in some schools females outperform males while in other schools males outperform females. In this case, the fixed effect of gender could be set to zero while the variance of the gender effect across schools would be estimated.

The vocabulary analysis in *Hierarchical Linear Models* supplies an example of a level-1 predictor having a random effect without a corresponding fixed effect. For the age interval under study, it was found that, on average, the linear effect of age was null. Yet this effect varied significantly across children. The level-1 model estimated was:

$$Y_{ti} = \pi_{1i}(age_{ti} - 12) + \pi_{2i}(age_{ti} - 12)^2 + e_{ti} \,.$$

However, the level-2 model was:

$$\pi_{1i} = r_{1i}$$
$$\pi_{2i} = \beta_{20} + r_{2i}$$

To implement this model we type the following lines in the command file:

```
level1:vocab=age12+age12sq+random
level2:age12=random
level2:age12sq=intrcpt2+random
```

Notice that age12 has a random effect but no fixed effect.

Constraints on the fixed effects

A researcher may wish to constrain two or more fixed effects to be equal. For example, Barnett, Marshall, Raudenbush, & Brennan (1993) applied this approach in studying correlates of psychological distress in married couples. Available for each person were two parallel measures of psychological distress. Hence, for each couple, there were four such measures (two per person). At level-1 these measures were modeled as the sum of a "true score" plus error:

$$Y_{ij} = \beta_{1j}X_{1ij} + \beta_{2j}X_{2j} + r_{ij} \,,$$

where X_{1ij} is an indicator for females, X_{2ij} is an indicator for males, and r_{ij} is a measurement error. Hence β_{1j} is the "true score" for females and β_{2j} is the "true score" for males. At level 2, these true scores are modeled as a function of predictor variables, one of which was marital role quality, W_j , a measure of one's satisfaction with one's marriage. (Note that this is also a model without a level-1 intercept.) A simple level-2 model is then:

$$\beta_{1j} = \gamma_{10} + \gamma_{11}W_j + u_{1j}$$
$$\beta_{2j} = \gamma_{20} + \gamma_{21}W_j + u_{2j} \,.$$

The four coefficients to be considered are

$$\gamma_{10}, \gamma_{11}, \gamma_{20}, \gamma_{21} \cdot$$

Suppose, we wish to specify that

$$\gamma_{11} = \gamma_{21} \cdot$$

In HLM/2L we assign the number 0 to those coefficients *not* to be constrained, and the number 1 to those being constrained. Thus, we would add the following line to the command file:

```
constrain:0,1,0,1
```

This procedure extends directly to multiple constraints. Suppose that the following coefficients were estimated

$$\gamma_{00}, \gamma_{01}, \gamma_{02}, \gamma_{10}, \gamma_{11}, \gamma_{12} \,,$$

and suppose the following line were typed into the command file:

```
constrain:0,1,2,0,1,2
```

Then the coefficients sharing the value of "1" would be constrained to be equal and the coefficients sharing the value of "2" would be constrained to be equal, with the result:

$$\gamma_{01} = \gamma_{11}, \quad \gamma_{02} = \gamma_{12} \cdot$$

Note, all coefficients sharing the value "0" are free to be estimated independently.

HLM/2L permits five different constraints to be specified in a single model. If you wish to specify the constraints while using the program in the interactive mode, add the line

```
constrain:y
```

to the command file. This will cause the appropriate prompts to be sent to the screen. That is:

```
Do you want to constrain any (more) of the gammas? Y

Do you want to constrain INTRCPT1/INTRCPT2, G00? N
Do you want to constrain         /  SECTOR, G01? N
Do you want to constrain         /    SIZE, G02? Y
Do you want to constrain    SES/INTRCPT2, G10? N
Do you want to constrain         /  SECTOR, G11? N
Do you want to constrain         /    SIZE, G12? Y

Do you wish to constrain any (more) of the gammas?  N
```

Here we have constrained G02 and G12 to the same value. (Note, this is only shown for illustrative purposes; this is not a particularly sensible constraint to introduce in this model.) If you answer "Y" in response to the prompt " Do you wish to constrain any (more) of the gammas?", the program will cycle back through the above prompts. The coefficients that have already been constrained, however, will no longer appear in the options list. The program listing below illustrates the HLM/2L output for this problem.

```
****************************************************************
*                                                              *
*      H   H  L      M    M   22                                *
*      H   H  L      MM MM   2  2                               *
*      HHHHH  L      M M M      2    Version 4.01               *
*      H   H  L      M    M     2                               *
*      H   H  LLLLL  M    M   2222                              *
*                                                              *
****************************************************************

SPECIFICATIONS FOR THIS HLM RUN                 Thu Feb  8 17:44:49 1996
--------------------------------------------------------------------------
    Problem Title: An example of a single constraint

    The data source for this run = hsb.ssm
    Output file name         = hsb4.lis
    The maximum number of level-2 units = 160
    The maximum number of iterations = 100
    Method of estimation: restricted maximum likelihood

Weighting Specification
-----------------------
                        Weight
                        Variable
            Weighting?  Name       Normalized?
Level 1       no                      no
Level 2       no                      no
```

The outcome variable is MATHACH

The model specified for the fixed effects was:
```
-------------------------------------------------------
    Level-1                Level-2         Specified
    Coefficients           Predictors      Constraints
---------------------      ---------------  -----------
        INTRCPT1, B0       INTRCPT2, G00        0
                           SECTOR, G01          0
                           SIZE, G02            1
 *      SES slope, B1      INTRCPT2, G10        0
                           SECTOR, G11          0
                           SIZE, G12            1
```

'*' – This level-1 predictor has been centered around its group mean.

The model specified for the covariance components was:
```
-----------------------------------------------------------
        Sigma—squared (constant across level-2 units)
        Tau dimensions
            INTRCPT1
                SES slope
```

Summary of the model specified (in equation format)
```
---------------------------------------------------
```

Level-1 Model

$$Y = B0 + B1*(SES) + R$$

Level-2 Model

$$B0 = G00 + G01*(SECTOR) + G02*(SIZE) + U0$$
$$B1 = G10 + G11*(SECTOR) + G12*(SIZE) + U1$$

The header page above illustrates HLM/2L output when a constraint on the level-2 coefficient is specified. We now skip ahead to display the final output page.

Final estimations of fixed effects:

Fixed Effect	Coefficient	Standard Error	T-ratio	P-value
For INTRCPT1, B0				
INTRCPT2, G00	11.160313	0.396005	28.182	0.000
SECTOR, G01	2.906368	0.452033	6.430	0.000
SIZE, G02	0.000173	0.000199	0.872	0.383
For SES slope, B1				
INTRCPT2, G10	2.571664	0.306898	8.380	0.000
SECTOR, G11	-1.245302	0.255402	-4.876	0.000

Some gammas have been constrained. See the table on page 1.

In this particular example, G02 and G12 were constrained to have the same value. That is, the estimated coefficient, standard error, and t-ratio for G12 are identical to the ones appearing in the table above for G02.

```
Final estimation of variance components:
-----------------------------------------------------------------------
Random Effect           Standard    Variance    df   Chi-square  P-value
                        Deviation   Component
-----------------------------------------------------------------------
INTRCPT1,       U0       2.58550      6.68479   157   1373.45726   0.000
   SES slope,   U1       0.45530      0.20729   157    174.96748   0.155
  level-1,      R        6.06157     36.74261
```

```
Statistics for current covariance components model
--------------------------------------------------
Deviance =  46662.38174
Number of estimated parameters =    4
```

Using design weights

In many studies, data arise from sample surveys in which units have been selected with known but unequal probabilities. In these cases it will often be desirable to weight observations in order to produce unbiased estimates of population parameters. According to standard practice in such cases, observations are weighted inversely proportional to their probability of selection.

For instance, suppose that in a pre-election poll, ethnic minority voters are oversampled to guarantee that various ethnic groups are represented in the sample. Without weighting, the over-sampled groups would exert undue influence on population estimates of the proportion of voters favoring a specific candidate. Using design weights produces unbiased population estimates. (Note: design weights may not be used in the nonlinear specification.)

Design weighting in the hierarchical context

When the data have a two-level hierarchical structure, several possibilities arise. Consider the problem of studying educational achievement in

U.S. high schools. A two-stage cluster sampling procedure will commonly be utilized in which schools are first sampled and then, within schools, students are selected. Over-sampling may occur at the school level, at the student level, or both. For example, schools might be stratified on the basis of region of the country, sector (public versus private) and location (urban versus suburban versus rural). Within schools, students may be stratified on the basis of grade or ethnicity. Selection of schools or students — or both — with unequal probability may be required to achieve the purposes of a study. How can the data be appropriately weighted to produce unbiased population estimates?

The appropriate weighting scheme will depend not only on the sampling plan but also on the conceptual orientation of the study. In some cases, researchers will aim to supply generalizations that apply to a population of level-1 units, *e.g.*, students. In other cases, the goal may be to make statements about the population of level-2 units, *e.g.*, schools. We shall consider implementation of weighting with HLM/2L for these two purposes.

Generalizing to a population of level-1 units

Suppose, the purpose of a study is to make inferences about a population of students (level-1 units). Suppose that these units have been sampled with unequal but known probability from the population of interest. The researcher may then wish to compute a design weight, that is, a level-1 variable taking on values inversely related to the probability of selection for each level-1 unit. Often the researcher will wish to normalize these weights in order to preserve the effective sample size. This is accomplished by multiplying them by a constant such that the sum of the weights is N, the total number of students. If P_{ij} is the probability of selection of student i in school j, one might compute

$$w_{ij} = \frac{N/P_{ij}}{\sum_{j=1}^{J}\sum_{i=1}^{n_j} 1/P_{ij}} \, , \qquad (2.1)$$

in which case

$$\sum_{j=1}^{J}\sum_{i=1}^{n_j} w_{ij} = N \, . \qquad (2.2)$$

Alternatively, HLM/2L will normalize weights supplied by the researcher. Either way, the researcher may ask HLM/2L to weight level-1 variables by w_{ij} so that the resulting parameter estimates will be unbiased with respect to parameters defined on the population of level-1 units.

Example of weighting for level-1 population estimates

During the creation of the SSM file, the user is prompted with two questions about level-1 and level-2 weighting. We illustrate this below in the context of a problem with level-1 weighting.

```
Is there a level-1 weighting variable?  Y
Will your generalizations principally involve level-1 effects
   or level-2 effects? (enter 1 or 2)  1
Are the level-1 weights already normalized?  N
What is the name of the level-1 weighting variable?  LEV1WT
Is there a level-2 weighting variable?  N
```

The program will now proceed with the remaining prompts to complete the construction of the SSM file. Note, the weighting options selected are directly incorporated into the computation of the sufficient statistics saved in the SSM file, and will be applied in every analysis using the SSM file. (The cover sheet of each HLM/2L output reminds the user of the weighting specification chosen during the SSM file creation.) If an alternative weighting scheme is desired (including the possibility of no weighting), the SSM file must be recreated accordingly.

Generalizing to a population of level-2 units

Simple random sample within level-2 units

Suppose now, the purpose of a study is to make inferences about a population of schools (level-2 units). Suppose that schools have been sampled with unequal but known probability from the population of interest while students have been sampled within schools according to a simple random sample. The researcher may then wish to compute a level-2 design weight, that is, a school-level variable having values inversely related to the probability of selection of the schools from the population of schools. The researcher may again wish to normalize these, that is, to multiply them by a constant such that the sum of the weights is J, the total number of schools. If P_j is the probability of selection of school j, one might compute

$$w_j = \frac{J/P_j}{\sum_{j=1}^{J} 1/P_j} ,$$

(2.3)

in which case

$$\sum_{j=1}^{J} w_j = J .$$

(2.4)

Again, HLM/2L will, as an option, normalize conventional design weights supplied by the researcher. Either way, the researcher may ask HLM/2L to weight level-2 variables by w_j so that the resulting parameter estimates will be unbiased with respect to parameters defined on the population of level-2 units.

Unequal probability of selection within level-2 units

In some cases level-2 units may first be selected with unequal probability from the population of all level-2 units. Then, within level-2 units, level-1 units are selected with unequal probability within each level-2 unit. Assuming that the purpose of a study is to make inferences about a population of level-2 units, the weighting problem becomes a bit more complex. In most cases (*e.g.*, in the case of the national survey data collected by the US National Center for Education Statistics) two types of weights will be available: school weights and student weights. HLM/2L enables the researcher simultaneously to use both types of weights to compute unbiased estimates of parameters defined on the population of schools.

The procedure works as follows. Again, consider the case of students nested within schools. First, the student data are weighted using level-1 weights that are normalized within each school. This weighting guarantees unbiased estimate of school-specific parameters. Also, school-level data are weighted by level-2 weights that are normalized across schools. This guarantees unbiased estimation over the population of schools.

Normalization of level-1 weights within schools works as follows. Within schools we compute

$$\omega_{ij} = \frac{n_j / w_{ij}}{\sum_{i=1}^{n_j} w_{ij}} \ , \tag{2.5}$$

where w_{ij} is, as before, the level-1 weight, guaranteeing that

$$\sum_{i=1}^{n_j} \omega_{ij} = n_j \ . \tag{2.6}$$

Then, the school weights are normalized as in Equation 2.3. The simultaneous use of both weights is required to guarantee unbiased estimation.

Example using weights at both levels

Again, the user is prompted with two questions about level-1 and level-2 weighting. We illustrate this below in the context of a problem with both level-1 and level-2 weighting.

```
Is there a level-1 weighting variable?  Y
Will your generalizations principally involve level-1 effects
   or level-2 effects? (enter 1 or 2)  2
Are the level-1 weights already normalized?  N
What is the name of the level-1 weighting variable?  LEV1WT
Is there a level-2 weighting variable?  Y
Are the level-2 weights already normalized?  N
What is the name of the level-2 weighting variable?  LEV2WT
```

Again, the program will now proceed with the remaining prompts to complete the construction of the SSM file. The cover sheet of each HLM/2L output reminds the user of the weighting specification chosen during the SSM file creation.

"V-Known" models

The V-known option of HLM/2L is a general routine which can be used for applications where the level-1 variances (and covariances) are known.

Included here are problems of meta-analysis (or research synthesis) and a wide range of other possible uses as discussed in Chapter 7 of *Hierarchical Linear Models*. The program input consists of Q random level-1 statistics for each group and their associated error variances and covariances.

We illustrate the use of the program with the data from the meta-analysis of teacher expectancy effects described on pp. 161–168 of *Hierarchical Linear Models*. The input data for this application are displayed below.

1	0.030	0.016	2.000
2	0.120	0.022	3.000
3	-0.140	0.028	3.000
4	1.180	0.139	0.000
5	0.260	0.136	0.000
6	-0.060	0.011	3.000
7	-0.020	0.011	3.000
8	-0.320	0.048	3.000
9	0.270	0.027	0.000
10	0.800	0.063	1.000
11	0.540	0.091	0.000
12	0.180	0.050	0.000
13	-0.020	0.084	1.000
14	0.230	0.084	2.000
15	-0.180	0.025	3.000
16	-0.060	0.028	3.000
17	0.300	0.019	1.000
18	0.070	0.009	2.000
19	-0.070	0.030	3.000

Data input format

Unlike the standard HLM/2L program, the V-known routine uses only a single data input file in ASCII format. It consists of the following information:

1. The first field is the unit ID in character format.
2. This is followed by the Q statistics from each unit. In the teacher expectancy effects meta-analysis Q equals one, the experiment effect size. (The effect size estimate appears in the third column of Table 7.1 in *Hierarchical Linear Models*.)
3. Next are the $Q(Q + 1)/2$ error variances and covariances associated with the set of Q statistics. These variance-covariance elements must be specified in row-column sequence from the lower triangle

of the matrix, *i.e.*, $V_{11}, V_{21}, V_{22}, \ldots, V_{Q,Q-1}, V_{Q,Q}$. For the meta-analysis application only a single error variance is needed. (Note the values in the third column above are the squares of the standard errors that appear in the fourth column of Table 7.1.)

4. Last are the potential level-2 predictor variables. In the teacher expectancy effects meta-analysis, there was only one predictor, the number of weeks of prior contact. (See column 2 of Table 7.1).

The Q statistics, their error variances and covariances, and the level-2 predictors must be ordered as described above and have a numeric format.

Creating the SSM file

We present below an example of an HLM/2L session that creates a sufficient statistics file using the V-known routine on the teacher expectancy effects data.

```
HLM2L

Will you be starting with raw data?  Y
Is the input file a v-known file?  Y

How many level-1 statistics are there?  1
How many level-2 predictors are there?  1

Enter 8 character name for level-1 statistic number 1:  EFFSIZE

Enter 8 character name for level-2 predictor number 1:  WEEKS

Input format of raw data file (the first field must be the character ID)
format:  (A2,3F12.3)
What file contains the data?  teacher.dat
Enter name of ssm file:  teacher.ssm

19 groups have been processed
```

The file, `teacher.dat`, contains the input data displayed above and the resulting sufficient statistics are saved in the `teacher.ssm` file. All subsequent analyses use `teacher.ssm`. Note that the input format has been specified for the character *id*, the level-1 statistic, *effsize*, the associated variance, and the level-2 predictor, *weeks*.

Estimating a V-known model

Once the SSM file has been created, it can be used to specify and estimate a variety of models as in any other HLM/2L application. The example below illustrates interactive use of the V-known program. (Batch mode is not available for the V-known program.)

HLM2L teacher.ssm

```
                        SPECIFYING AN HLM MODEL

Level-1 predictor variable specification

Which level-1 statistics do you wish to use?
The choices are:
 For  EFFSIZE enter  1

 level-1 statistic? (Enter 0 to end) 1

Level-2 predictor variable specification

Which level-2 variables do you wish to use?
The choices are:
 For    WEEKS enter  1

 Level-2 predictor? (Enter 0 to end) 1

                        OUTPUT SPECIFICATION

How many iterations do you want to do? 300
 Enter a problem title: Teacher expectancy meta-analysis
 Enter name of output file: teacher.lis
Computing . . ., please wait
```

```
        ***********************************************************
        *                                                         *
        *       H   H  L       M   M   22                         *
        *       H   H  L       MM MM  2  2                        *
        *       HHHHH  L       M M M    2      Version 4.01       *
        *       H   H  L       M   M   2                          *
        *       H   H  LLLLL   M   M   2222                       *
        *                                                         *
        ***********************************************************

   SPECIFICATIONS FOR THIS HLM RUN              Thu Feb  8 18:06:09 1996

   ----------------------------------------------------------------------
    Problem Title: teacher expectancy meta-analysis
```

```
The data source for this run = teacher.ssm
Output file name          = teacher.lis
The maximum number of level-2 units = 19
The maximum number of iterations = 300
Method of estimation: restricted maximum likelihood
Note: this is a v-known analysis
```

The model specified for the fixed effects was:
```
-------------------------------------------------------
     Level-1                 Level-2
     Effects                 Predictors
---------------------    ----------------
         EFFSIZE, B1       INTRCPT2, G10
                            WEEKS, G11
```

The model specified for the covariance components was:
```
----------------------------------------------------------
        Variance(s and covariances) at level-1 externally specified
        Tau dimensions
             EFFSIZE
```

Summary of the model specified (in equation format)
```
----------------------------------------------------
Level-1 Model

        Y1 = B1 + E1

Level-2 Model

        B1 = G10 + G11*(WEEKS) + U1
```

Starting Values
```
---------------
 Tau(0)
   EFFSIZE      0.02004
```

Estimation of fixed effects
(Based on starting values of covariance components)

Fixed Effect	Coefficient	Standard Error	T-ratio	P-value
For EFFSIZE, B1				
INTRCPT2, G10	0.433737	0.109700	3.954	0.001
WEEKS, G11	-0.168572	0.046563	-3.620	0.002

```
The value of the likelihood function at iteration 1 = -3.414348E+01
The value of the likelihood function at iteration 2 = -3.350241E+01
```

```
The value of the likelihood function at iteration 3 = -3.301695E+01
The value of the likelihood function at iteration 4 = -3.263749E+01
The value of the likelihood function at iteration 5 = -3.121675E+01
  .
  .
  .
The value of the likelihood function at iteration 296 = -2.984029E+01
The value of the likelihood function at iteration 297 = -2.984020E+01
The value of the likelihood function at iteration 298 = -2.984010E+01
The value of the likelihood function at iteration 299 = -2.984000E+01

******* ITERATION 300 *******

  Tau
   EFFSIZE        0.00015

  Tau (as correlations)
   EFFSIZE   1.000


  ----------------------------------------------------
  Random level-1 coefficient   Reliability estimate
  ----------------------------------------------------
   EFFSIZE, B1                        0.006

The value of the likelihood function at iteration 300 = -2.983990E+01


Final estimations of fixed effects:
-----------------------------------------------------------------------
    Fixed Effect      Coefficient   Standard Error   T-ratio   P-value
-----------------------------------------------------------------------
For          EFFSIZE, B1
   INTRCPT2, G10       0.408847        0.087358        4.680    0.000
     WEEKS, G11       -0.158080        0.036040       -4.386    0.000


Final estimation of variance components:
-----------------------------------------------------------------------
Random Effect            Standard    Variance    df   Chi-square   P-value
                         Deviation   Component
-----------------------------------------------------------------------
 EFFSIZE,      U1         0.01209     0.00015    17    16.53615    >.500


Statistics for current covariance components model
--------------------------------------------------
Deviance =      59.67980
Number of estimated parameters =     2
```

In general, the HLM/2L results for this example closely approximate the more traditional results that would be obtained from a graphical exami-

nation of the likelihood function. (For this particular model, the likelihood mode is at zero.) Note, the value of the likelihood was still changing after 300 iterations. Often, HLM/2L converges after a relatively small number of iterations. When the number of iterations required is large, as in this case, this indicates that the estimation is moving toward a boundary condition. (In this example it is a variance estimate of zero for Tau.) This can be seen by comparing the starting value estimate for Tau, 0.020, with the final estimate of 0.00015. (For a further discussion see p. 202 of *Hierarchical Linear Models*.)

3

Conceptual and Statistical Background for Three-Level Models

The models estimated by HLM/3L are applicable to hierarchical data structure with three levels of random variation in which the errors of prediction at each level can be assumed approximately normally distributed. Consider, for example, a study in which achievement test scores are collected from a sample of children nested within classrooms that are in turn nested within schools. This data structure is hierarchical (each child belongs to one and only one classroom and each classroom belongs to one and only one school); and there are three levels of random variation: variation among children within classrooms, variation among classroom within schools, and variation among schools. The outcome (achievement test scores) makes the normality assumption at level 1 reasonable, and the normality assumption at the classroom and school levels will often also be a sensible one.

Chapter 8 of *Hierarchical Linear Models* discusses several applications of a three-level model. The first is a three-level cross-sectional study as described above. A second case involves time-series data collected on each subject where the subjects are nested within organizations. This latter example is from the Sustaining Effects Study, where achievement data were collected at five time points for each child. Here the time-series data are nested within children and the children are nested within schools. A third example in Chapter 8 involves measures taken on each of the multiple classes taught by secondary school teachers. The classes are nested within teachers and the teachers within schools. A final example involves multiple items from a questionnaire administered to teachers. The items vary "within teachers" at level 1, the teachers vary within schools at level 2, and the schools vary at level 3. In effect, the level-1 model is a model for the measurement error associated with the questionnaire. Clearly, there are many interesting applications of a three-level model.

The general three-level model

The three-level model consists of three submodels, one for each level. For example, if the research problem consists of data on students nested within classrooms and classrooms within schools, the level-1 model will represent the relationships among the student-level variables, the level-2 model will capture the influence of class-level factors, and the level-3 model will incorporate school-level effects. Formally there are $i = 1, \ldots,$ n_{jk} level-1 units (*e.g.*, students), which are nested within each of $j = 1, \ldots, J_k$ level-2 units (*e.g.*, classrooms), which in turn are nested within each of $k = 1, \ldots, K$ level-3 units (*e.g.*, schools).

Level-1 model

In the level-1 model we represent the outcome for case i within level-2 unit j and level-3 unit k as:

$$
\begin{aligned}
Y_{ijk} &= \pi_{0jk} + \pi_{1jk}a_{1ijk} + \pi_{2jk}a_{2ijk} + \cdots + \pi_{pjk}a_{pijk} + e_{ijk} \\
&= \pi_{0jk} + \sum_{p=1}^{P} \pi_{pjk}a_{pijk} + e_{ijk} ,
\end{aligned}
\tag{3.1}
$$

where

π_{pjk} $(p = 0, 1, \ldots, P)$ are *level-1 coefficients*,

a_{pijk} is *level-1 predictor p* for case i in level-2 unit j and level-3 unit k,

e_{ijk} is the *level-1 random effect*, and

σ^2 is the variance of e_{ijk}, that is the *level-1 variance*.

Here we assume that the random term $e_{ijk} \sim N(0, \sigma^2)$.

Level-2 model

Each of the π_{pjk} coefficients in the level-1 model becomes an outcome variable in the level-2 model:

$$
\begin{aligned}
\pi_{pjk} &= \beta_{p0k} + \beta_{p1k}X_{1jk} + \beta_{p2k}X_{2jk} + \cdots + \beta_{pQ_pk}X_{Q_pjk} + r_{pjk} \\
&= \beta_{p0k} + \sum_{q=1}^{Q_p} \beta_{pqk}X_{qjk} + r_{pjk} ,
\end{aligned}
\tag{3.2}
$$

where

β_{pqk} $(q = 0, 1, \ldots, Q_p)$ are *level-2 coefficients*,

X_{qjk} is a *level-2 predictor*, and

r_{pjk} is a *level-2 random effect*.

We assume that, for each unit j, the vector $(r_{0jk}, r_{1jk}, \ldots, r_{Pjk})'$ is distributed as multivariate normal with each element having a mean of zero and where the variance of r_{pjk} is:

$$
\mathsf{Var}(r_{pjk}) = \tau_{\pi pp} .
\tag{3.3}
$$

For any pair of random effects p and p',

$$
\mathsf{Cov}(r_{pjk}, r_{p'jk}) = \tau_{\pi pp'} .
$$

These *level-2 variance and covariance components* can be collected into a dispersion matrix, $\mathbf{T}_\pi$, whose maximum dimension is $(P+1) \times (P+1)$.

We note that each level-1 coefficient can be modeled at level-2 as one of three general forms:

1. *a level-1 coefficient that is fixed at the same value for all level-2 units*; e.g.,

$$
\pi_{pjk} = \beta_{p0k} ,
\tag{3.4}
$$

2. *a level-1 coefficient that varies non-randomly among level-2 units,* e.g.,

$$
\pi_{pjk} = \beta_{p0k} + \sum_{q=1}^{Q_p} \beta_{pqk}X_{qjk} ,
\tag{3.5}
$$

3. *a level-1 coefficient that varies randomly among level-2 units, e.g.,*

$$\pi_{pjk} = \beta_{p0k} + r_{pjk} \tag{3.6}$$

or

$$\pi_{pjk} = \beta_{p0k} + \sum_{q=1}^{Q_p} \beta_{pqk} X_{qjk} + r_{pjk} . \tag{3.7}$$

The actual dimension of T_π in any application depends on the number of level-1 coefficients specified as randomly varying. We also note that a different set of level-2 predictors may be used in each of the $P + 1$ equations that form the level-2 model.

Level-3 model

Each of the level-2 coefficients, β_{pqk}, defined in the level-2 model, becomes an outcome variable in the level-3 model:

$$\begin{aligned} \beta_{pqk} &= \gamma_{pq0} + \gamma_{pq1}W_{1k} + \gamma_{pq2}W_{2k} + \cdots + \gamma_{pqS_{pq}}W_{S_{pq}k} + u_{pqk} \\ &= \gamma_{pq0} + \sum_{s=1}^{S_{pq}} \gamma_{pqs}W_{sk} + u_{pqk} , \end{aligned} \tag{3.8}$$

where

γ_{pqs} $(s = 0, 1, \ldots, S_{pq})$ are *level-3 coefficients*,

W_{sk} is a *level-3 predictor*, and

u_{pqk} is a *level-3 random effect*.

We assume that, for each level-3 unit, the vector of level-3 random effects (the u_{pqk}'s) is distributed as multivariate normal, with each having a mean of zero and with covariance matrix T_β, whose maximum dimension is:

$$\sum_{p=0}^{p}(Q_p + 1) \times \sum_{p=0}^{p}(Q_p + 1) .$$

We note that each level-2 coefficient can be modeled at level-3 as one of three general forms:

1. *as a fixed effect, e.g.,*

$$\beta_{pqk} = \gamma_{pq0} \, , \qquad\qquad (3.9)$$

2. *as non-randomly varying, e.g.,*

$$\beta_{pqk} = \gamma_{pq0} + \sum_{s=1}^{S_{pq}} \gamma_{pqs} W_{sk} \, , \qquad\qquad (3.10)$$

3. *as random varying, e.g.,*

$$\beta_{pqk} = \gamma_{pq0} + u_{pqk} \qquad\qquad (3.11)$$

or

$$\beta_{pqk} = \gamma_{pq0} + \sum_{s=1}^{S_{pq}} \gamma_{pqs} W_{sk} + u_{pqk} \, . \qquad\qquad (3.12)$$

The actual dimension of T_β in any application depends on the number of level-3 coefficients specified as randomly varying. We also note that a different set of level-3 predictors may be used in each equation of the level-3 model.

Parameter estimation

Three kinds of parameter estimates are available in a three-level model: empirical Bayes estimates of randomly varying level-1 and level-2 coefficients; maximum-likelihood estimates of the level-3 coefficients (note: these are also generalized least squares estimates); and maximum-likelihood estimates of the variance-covariance components. The maximum-likelihood estimate of the level-3 coefficients and the variance-covariance components are printed on the output for every run. The empirical Bayes estimates for the level-1 and level-2 coefficients may optionally be saved in the "residual files" at levels 2 and 3, respectively. Reliability estimates for each random level-1 and level-2 coefficient are always produced.

The actual estimation procedure for the three-level model differs a bit from the default two-level model. By default, HLM/2L uses a "restricted maximum likelihood" approach in which the variance-covariance components are estimated by means of maximum likelihood and then the fixed effects (level-2 coefficients) are estimated via generalized least squares given those variance-covariance estimates. In HLM/3L, not only the variance-covariance components, but also the fixed effects (level-3 coefficients) are estimated by means of maximum likelihood. This procedure is referred to as "full" as opposed to "restricted" maximum likelihood. (For a further discussion of this see *Hierarchical Linear Models*, pp. 44-48. The actual computational formulas appear on pp. 245–248.) Note, full maximum-likelihood is also now available as an option for HLM/2L.

Hypothesis testing

As in the case of the two-level program, the three-level program routinely prints standard errors and t-tests for each of the level-3 coefficients ("the fixed effects") as well as a chi-square test of homogeneity for each random effect. In addition, optional "multivariate hypothesis tests" are available in the three-level program. Multivariate tests for the level-3 coefficients enable both omnibus tests and specific comparisons of the parameter estimates just as described in the section *Multivariate hypothesis tests for fixed effects* on page 54. Multivariate tests regarding alternative variance-covariance structures at level 2 or level 3 proceed just as in the section *Multivariate tests of variance-covariance components specification* on page 56.

The use of full maximum likelihood for parameter estimation in HLM/3L has a consequence for hypothesis testing. In both the two- and the three-level analyses, one can test alternative variance-covariance structures by means of the likelihood-ratio test as described in the section *Multivariate tests of variance-covariance components specification* on page 56. However, in the case of the three-level model it is also possible to test alternative specifications of the fixed (level-3) coefficients by means of a likelihood-ratio test. In fact, any pair of nested three-level models can be compared using the likelihood-ratio test. By nested models, we refer to a pair of models in which the more complex model includes all of the parameters of the simpler model plus one or more additional parameters.

4   Working with HLM/3L

As in the case of the two-level program, data analysis by means of the HLM/3L program will typically involve three stages:

1. Construction of an SSM file (the sufficient statistics matrix)
2. Execution of analyses based on the SSM file
3. Evaluation of fitted models based on residual files

As in HLM/2L, HLM/3L analyses can be executed in Windows, interactive, and batch modes. We describe an interactive execution below. We then consider batch execution. Finally, we consider a number of special options. (For Windows implementation, see the help facility in the HLM/3L for Windows program.)

An example using HLM/3L in interactive mode

Chapter 8 in *Hierarchical Linear Models* presents a series of analyses of data from the US *Sustaining Effects Study*, a longitudinal study of children's growth in academic achievement during the primary years. A level-1 model specifies the relationship between age and academic achievement for each child. At level 2, the coefficients describing each child's growth vary across children within schools as a function of demographic variables. At level 3, the parameters that describe the distribution of growth curves within each school vary across schools as a function of school-level predictors.

To illustrate the operation of the HLM/3L program, we analyze another data set having a similar structure. The level-1 data are time-series observations on 1721 students nested within 60 urban public primary schools and mathematics achievement is the outcome. These data are provided along with the HLM software so that users may replicate our results in order to assure that the program is operating correctly.

Constructing the SSM file from raw data

The user has the same range of options for data input for HLM/3L as for HLM/2L (see page 13). We first illustrate the use of ASCII data files and then consider SYSTAT, SAS, and other file inputs.

The SSM file is written in binary format for efficient storage and computation and therefore cannot be interpreted by the human eye. However, the user can execute the PRSSM3 sub-program in order to examine the contents of the SSM file. To execute this sub-program, simply type at the system prompt:

PRSSM3 *ssmfile*

(where *ssmfile* can be replaced by the SSM filename of the user's choice). This will translate the SSM file into ASCII format and store it in a file called *ssmfile*.OUT for subsequent review. To override the output filename, specify a filename as a second parameter on the command line, for example, OUTPUT:

PRSSM3 *ssmfile* OUTPUT

ASCII input

Data input requires a level-1 file (in our illustration a time-series data file), a level-2 file (child-level file), and a level-3 (school level) file.

Level-1 file.   The level-1 file, eg1.dat, has 7242 observations collected on 1721 children beginning at the end of grade one and followed up annually thereafter until grade six. There are four level-1 variables (not including the *school id* and the *child id*). Time-series data for the first two children are printed below. There are eight records listed, three for the first child and five for the second. (Typically there are four or five observations per child with a maximum of six.) The first field is the level-3 (*i.e.*, school) id and the second field is the level-2 (*i.e.*, child) id. We see that the first record comes from school 2020 and child 273026452 within that school. Notice that this child has three records, one for each of three measurement occasions. Following the two id fields are that child's values on four variables:

  □ *year* (year of the study minus 3.5)

   This variable can take on values of −2.5, −1.5, −0.5, 0.5, 1.5, and 2.5 for the six years of data collection.

  □ *grade*

   The grade level minus 1.0 of the child at each testing occasion. Therefore, it is 0 at grade 1, 1.0 at grade 2, etc.

  □ *math*

   A math test in an IRT scale score metric.

  □ *retained*

   An indicator that a child is retained in grade for a particular year (1 = retained, 0 = not retained).

We see that the first child, child 27306452 in school 2020 had values of 0.5, 1.5, and 2.5 on *year*. Clearly, that child had no data at the first three data collection waves (because we see no values of −2.5, −1.5, or −0.5 on *year*), but did have data at the last three waves. We see also that this child was not retained in grade during this period since the values for *grade* increase by 1 each year and since *retained* takes on a value of 0 for each year. The three *math* scores of that child (1.146, 1.134, 2.300) show no growth in time period 1.5. Oddly enough, the time-series record for the second child (child 273030991 in school 2020) displays a similar pattern in the same testing.

```
2020 273026452   0.5  2.0  1.146 0
2020 273026452   1.5  3.0  1.134 0
2020 273026452   2.5  4.0  2.300 0
2020 273030991  -1.5  0.0 -1.303 0
2020 273030991  -0.5  1.0  0.439 0
2020 273030991   0.5  2.0  2.430 0
2020 273030991   1.5  3.0  2.254 0
2020 273030991   2.5  4.0  3.873 0
```

The format of the data is $(\text{A4},\text{1X},\text{A9},\text{1X},\text{2F5.1},\text{F7.3},\text{F2.0})$, with the two id fields formatted alphanumeric followed by four numeric fields for the variables. *The id fields in HLM/2L and HLM/3L must be formatted alphanumeric. In HLM/3L, the first and second ID fields must always contain the level-3 and level-2 id's, respectively. These two fields must have the same format in both the level-1 and level-2 files.*

The level-1 and level-2 files must also be sorted in the same order of level-2 id nested within level-3 id, e.g., children within schools. If this nested sorting is not performed, an incorrect sufficient statistics file will result.

Level-2 file.   The level-2 units in the illustration are 1721 children. The data are stored in the file eg2.dat. The level-2 data for the first ten children are listed below. The first field is the *school id* and the second is the *child id*. Note that each of the first ten children is in school 2020. There are three variables:

- ❑ *gender* (1 = female, 0 = male)
- ❑ *black* (1 = African-American, 0 = other)
- ❑ *hispanic* (1= Hispanic, 0 = other)

We see, for example, that child 273026452 is an Hispanic male (*gender* = 0, *black* = 0, *hispanic* = 1).

```
2020 273026452 0 0 1
2020 273030991 0 0 0
2020 273059461 0 0 1
2020 278058841 0 0 0
2020 292017571 0 0 1
2020 292020281 0 0 0
2020 292020361 0 0 0
2020 292025081 0 0 0
2020 292026211 1 0 0
2020 292027291 1 0 1
```

The format for level-2 file is (A4,1X,A9,3F2.0). Notice that, as required, the first two fields of the level-2 file are the same as those in the level-1 file and that the level-2 data are sorted as in the level-1 file.

Level-3 file. The level-3 units in the illustration are 60 schools. Level-3 data for the first ten schools are printed below. The full data are in the file eg3.dat. The first field on the left is the *school-id*. There are three level-3 variables:

- ❏ *size* (number of students enrolled in the school)
- ❏ *lowinc* (the percent of students from low income families)
- ❏ *mobile* (the percent of students moving during the course of a single academic year)

The first field on the left is the level-3 id. The format for these data is (A4,1X,3F7.1).

We see that the first school, school 2020 has 380 students, 40.3% of whom are low income. The school mobility rate is 12.5%.

```
2020    380.0    40.3    12.5
2040    502.0    83.1    18.6
2180    777.0    96.6    44.4
2330    800.0    78.9    31.7
2340   1133.0    93.7    67.0
2380    439.0    36.9    39.3
2390    566.0   100.0    39.9
2440    767.0    44.8    37.1
2480    113.0    59.3    25.8
2520    828.0    76.9    10.5
```

In sum, there are four variables at level 1, three at level 2 and three at level 3. Note, the id's do not count as variables. Once the user is clear on the number of variables in each file, the format of each file, the variable names, and the filenames, creation of the SSM file is exactly analogous to the procedure described in the section *Constructing the SSM file from raw data* on page 9 for the two-level program. The program can handle missing data at level-1 only, with the same options available as discussed in HLM/2L. The three-level program only handles level-1 design weights at this time.

Example: constructing an SSM file for the urban public school data. User responses appear in a swiss font; additional explanatory comments are in *italic*.

```
Will you be starting with raw data? Y
Enter the type of raw data:
    for ASCII input         enter 1
    for SYSTAT.SYS file      enter 2
    for SAS transport file   enter 3
    for other file types     enter 4
    Type? 1
```

```
Input number of level-1 variables (not including the character ID): 4
The first field must be a character level-3 id, the second, the level-2 id
Input format of level-1 file: (A4,1X,A9,1X,2F5.1,F7.3,F2.0)
```

```
Input name of level-1 file: EG1.DAT
```

```
Input number of level-2 variables (not including the character ID): 3
The first field must be a character level-3 id, the second, the level-2 id
Input format of level-2 file: (A4,1X,A9,3F2.0)
Input name of level-2 file: EG2.DAT
```

```
Input number of level-3 variables (not including the character ID): 3
The first field must be a character level-3 id
Input format of level-3 file: (A4,1X,3F7.1)
Input name of level-3 file: EG3.DAT
```

```
Enter 8 character name for level-1 variable number 1: YEAR
Enter 8 character name for level-1 variable number 2: GRADE
Enter 8 character name for level-1 variable number 3: MATH
Enter 8 character name for level-1 variable number 4: RETAINED
```

```
Enter 8 character name for level-2 variable number 1: GENDER
Enter 8 character name for level-2 variable number 2: BLACK
Enter 8 character name for level-2 variable number 3: HISPANIC
```

```
Enter 8 character name for level-3 variable number 1: SIZE
Enter 8 character name for level-3 variable number 2: LOWINC
Enter 8 character name for level-3 variable number 3: MOBILE
```

```
Is there missing data in the level-1 file? N
Is there a level-1 weighting variable? N
```

```
Enter name of ssm file: EG.SSM
```

After the SSM file is computed, descriptive statistics for each file are sent to the screen. **It is important to examine these carefully to guarantee that no errors were made in specifying the format of the data.** *HLM/3L will also ask if the user wishes to save these in a file,* named HLM3SSM.STS. *These results are helpful as a reference and when constructing a descriptive table about the data for a written report.*

LEVEL-1 DESCRIPTIVE STATISTICS

VARIABLE NAME	N	MEAN	SD	MINIMUM	MAXIMUM
YEAR	7242	0.38	1.40	-2.50	2.50
GRADE	7242	1.81	1.35	0.00	5.00
MATH	7242	-0.54	1.54	-5.22	5.77
RETAINED	7242	0.05	0.22	0.00	1.00

LEVEL-2 DESCRIPTIVE STATISTICS

VARIABLE NAME	N	MEAN	SD	MINIMUM	MAXIMUM
GENDER	1721	0.51	0.50	0.00	1.00
BLACK	1721	0.69	0.46	0.00	1.00
HISPANIC	1721	0.15	0.35	0.00	1.00

LEVEL-3 DESCRIPTIVE STATISTICS

VARIABLE NAME	N	MEAN	SD	MINIMUM	MAXIMUM
SIZE	60	642.53	317.37	113.00	1486.00
LOWINC	60	73.74	27.27	0.00	100.00
MOBILE	60	34.74	13.21	8.80	67.00

SYSTAT or SAS file input

Construction of the SSM file from SYSTAT system files or SAS V5 transport files is simpler than from ASCII because no format statements are needed. The user simply selects the desired variables from the specified SYSTAT system files or SAS V5 transport files as was previously illustrated in HLM/2L (section *SYSTAT file input* on page 19). The only difference with HLM/3L is that three system files, one for each level, must now be specified. The level-1 and level-2 files must include for each record the appropriate level-2 and level-3 ids. The level-3 file must include the level-3 id corresponding to each record. *Each file must be sorted by id field following the same procedures as previously described for ASCII data input.*

Other file type input

HLM/3L has the same range of options for data input as HLM/2L. In addition to SYSTAT and SAS, the PC implementation allows numerous other data formats from, for example, SPSS, STATA, EXCEL, and LOTUS input. See page 13 for details.

Executing analyses based on the SSM file

Once the SSM file is constructed, model fitting analyses use this SSM file as input. Model specification via the interactive mode has five steps:

Step 1: Specification of the level-1 model. In our case we shall model mathematics achievement (*math*) as the outcome, to be predicted by *year* in the study. Hence, the level-1 model will have two coefficients for each child: the intercept and the *year* slope.

Step 2: Specification of the level-2 prediction model. Here each level-1 coefficient — the intercept and the *year* slope in our example — becomes an outcome variable. We may select certain child characteristics to predict each of these level-1 coefficients. In principle, the level-2 parameters then describe the distribution of growth curves within each school.

Step 3: Specification of level-1 coefficients as random or non-random across level-two units. We shall model the intercept and the *year* slope as varying randomly across the children within schools.

Step 4: Specification of the level-3 prediction model. Here each level-2 coefficient becomes an outcome, and we can select level-3 variables to predict school-to-school variation in these level-2 coefficients. In principle, this model specifies how schools differ with respect to the distribution of growth curves within them.

Step 5: Specification of the level-2 coefficients as random or non-random across level-3 units.

The interactive program also poses a number of questions about output options and additional procedures. We comment on these as they arise in the computer session reproduced below.

Once the program begins to iterate, HLM/3L will continue to do so until either convergence has been achieved or the maximum number of iterations specified — whichever comes first. If you wish to terminate the computations early, press the Ctrl–C key combination *once*. This will stop the analyses after the current iteration and provide a full presentation of results based on that iteration. *If you press Ctrl–C more than once, however, computation is terminated and all output is lost.*

HLM3L EG.SSM   *(issue the program name at the system prompt to start)*

As in HLM/2L, the first argument, HLM3L, *tells the computer to execute the three-level HLM program; the second argument specifies the SSM file to be analyzed. An optional third argument specifies a command file that can be used to automate aspects of model specification via batch-mode (see the section "Using HLM/3L in batch mode" on page 102).*

```
                SPECIFYING A LEVEL-1 OUTCOME VARIABLE

Please specify a level-1 outcome variable
The choices are:
 For     YEAR enter  1    For    GRADE enter  2    For     MATH enter  3
 For RETAINED enter  4

What is the outcome variable:  3



                   SPECIFYING AN HLM MODEL

Level-1 predictor variable specification

Which level-1 predictors do you wish to use?
The choices are:
 For     YEAR enter  1    For    GRADE enter  2
 For RETAINED enter  4

level-1 predictor? (Enter 0 to end)  1
level-1 predictor? (Enter 0 to end)  0

Do you want to center any level-1 predictors?  N
```

If you answer "Y" here, the program will offer the option of centering each predictor around the unit mean, $a_{.jk}$, or the grand mean, $a_{...}$.

Do you want to set the level-1 intercept to zero in this
analysis? **N**

This allows you to formulate a model with no intercept term at level 1.

Level-2 predictor variable specification

Which level-2 variables do you wish to use?

The choices are:
  For   GENDER enter 1   For   BLACK enter 2   For HISPANIC enter 3

Which level-2 predictor to model INTRCPT1, P0?
 Level-2 predictor? (Enter 0 to end) **0**
Which level-2 predictor to model   YEAR, P1 slope?
 Level-2 predictor? (Enter 0 to end) **0**

Do you want to set the level-2 intercept to zero in this analysis? **N**

This allows you to formulate a model with no intercept term at level 2.

Do you want to constrain the variances in any of the level-2 random
effect to zero? **N**

*If you answer "Y" here, HLM/3L will allow you to fix one or more level-
2 variances (and associated covariances) to zero. Through this process
the corresponding level-2 outcome is specified as fixed (no predictors) or
non-randomly varying (some predictors included.) Notice that the model
above contains no level-2 predictors. Had level-2 predictors been included,
the user would have been prompted about possible centering options. The
choices are: centering about the group mean, $X_{\cdot k}$, grand mean, $X_{\cdot\cdot}$, or no
centering.*

Level-3 predictor variable specification

Which level-3 predictors do you wish to use?

The choices are:
  For   SIZE   enter 1   For LOWINC enter 2   For MOBILE enter 3

Which level-3 predictors to model INTRCPT1/INTRCPT2, B00?
 Level-3 predictor? (Enter 0 to end) **0**
Which level-3 predictors to model   YEAR/INTRCPT2, B10 slope?
 Level-3 predictor? (Enter 0 to end) **0**

Notice also that this model contains no level-3 predictors. Had level-3 predictors been included, the user would have been prompted about possible centering options. The choices are: centering about the grand mean, W., or no centering.

```
Do you want to constrain the variances in any of the level-3 random
  effect to zero? N
```

By answering "Y" here, you can specify level-3 outcomes as fixed or non-randomly varying.

```
                        ADDITIONAL PROGRAM FEATURES

Select the level-2 variables that you might consider for
inclusion as predictors in subsequent models.

The choices are:
 For   GENDER enter  1    For     BLACK enter  2    For HISPANIC enter  3

Which level-2 variables to model INTRCPT1, P0?
 Level-2 predictor? (Enter 0 to end) 1
 Level-2 predictor? (Enter 0 to end) 2
 Level-2 predictor? (Enter 0 to end) 3

Which level-2 variables to model     YEAR, P1 slope?
 Level-2 predictor? (Enter 0 to end) -1
```

As in HLM/2L, HLM/3L will interpret the response of "-1" to repeat the selections made for the previous prompt, i.e., 1,2,3.

```
Select the level-3 predictor variables that you might consider for
inclusion as predictors in subsequent models.

The choices are:
 For    SIZE  enter  1    For LOWINC enter  2    For  MOBILE enter  3

Which level-3 variables to model INTRCPT1/INTRCPT2, B00?
 Level-3 predictor? (Enter 0 to end) 1
 Level-3 predictor? (Enter 0 to end) 2
 Level-3 predictor? (Enter 0 to end) 3

Which level-3 variables to model     YEAR/INTRCPT2, B10 slope?
 Level-3 predictor? (Enter 0 to end) -1

Do you wish to use any of the optional hypothesis testing
procedures? N
```

The options available here are a multivariate hypothesis test for the fixed effects and Likelihood Ratio Test for comparison of nested models.

```
                          OUTPUT SPECIFICATION

How many iterations do you want to do?  200
Enter a problem title:  Unconditional Linear Growth Model
Enter name of output file:  eg1.lis

Computing . . ., please wait
Starting values computed.  Iterations begun.

The value of the likelihood function at iteration 1 = -8.176168E+003
The value of the likelihood function at iteration 2 = -8.171976E+003
The value of the likelihood function at iteration 3 = -8.171606E+003
The value of the likelihood function at iteration 4 = -8.171439E+003
The value of the likelihood function at iteration 5 = -8.171301E+003
.
.
.
The value of the likelihood function at iteration 9 = -8.169538E+003
The value of the likelihood function at iteration 10 = -8.169381E+003
The value of the likelihood function at iteration 11 = -8.169532E+003
The value of the likelihood function at iteration 12 = -8.169532E+003
The value of the likelihood function at iteration 13 = -8.169532E+003
```

An annotated example of HLM/3L output

Here is the output produced by the interactive session described above. HLM/3L stored this in the file specified by the user with the name eg1.lis.

```
******************************************************************
*                                                                *
*      HH    HH  LL        MM      MM    333                      *
*      HH    HH  LL        MMM    MMM   33333                     *
*      HH    HH  LL        MMMM  MMMM  33   33                    *
*      HHHHHHHH  LL        MM MMM MM        33                    *
*      HHHHHHHH  LL        MM  M  MM        33                    *
*      HH    HH  LL        MM      MM   33  33                    *
*      HH    HH  LLLLLLLL  MM      MM   33333                     *
*      HH    HH  LLLLLLLL  MM      MM    333                      *
*                  Version 4.01                                   *
******************************************************************
SPECIFICATIONS FOR THIS HLM RUN            Mon Feb  5 14:15:06 1996
```

The first page of the output gives the specification of the model.

Problem Title: Unconditional Linear Growth Model

The data source for this run = eg.ssm
Output file name   = eg1.lis
The maximum number of level-2 units = 1721
The maximum number of level-3 units = 60
The maximum number of iterations = 200
Method of estimation: full maximum likelihood

Name of the SSM file
Name of this output file
There are 1721 children
There are 60 schools

Weighting Specification

	Weighting?	Weight Variable Name	Normalized?
Level 1	no		no

The outcome variable is   MATH

The model specified for the fixed effects was:

Level-1 Coefficients	Level-2 Predictors	Level-3 Predictors
INTRCPT1, P0	INTRCPT2, B00	INTRCPT3, G000
YEAR slope, P1	INTRCPT2, B10	INTRCPT3, G100

Summary of the model specified (in equation format)

Level-1 Model

$$Y = P0 + P1*(YEAR) + E$$

Level-2 Model

$$P0 = B00 + R0$$
$$P1 = B10 + R1$$

Level-3 Model

$$B00 = G000 + U0$$
$$B10 = G100 + U1$$

Next come the initial parameter estimates or "starting values." Users should not base inferences on these values, the sole purpose of which is to get the iterations started.

For starting values, data from 7242 level-1 and 1721 level-2 records were used.

STARTING VALUES

Sigma-squared(0) =   0.29630

```
Tau(pi)(0)
   INTRCPT1,P0      0.71180        0.05116
       YEAR,P1      0.05116        0.01605

Tau(beta)(0)
   INTRCPT1           YEAR
   INTRCPT2,B00 INTRCPT2,B10
       0.14935        0.01469
       0.01469        0.01197
```

The value of the likelihood function at iteration 1 = -8.176168E+003
The value of the likelihood function at iteration 2 = -8.171976E+003
The value of the likelihood function at iteration 3 = -8.171606E+003
The value of the likelihood function at iteration 4 = -8.171439E+003
The value of the likelihood function at iteration 5 = -8.171301E+003
                                                  .
                                                  .
                                                  .
The value of the likelihood function at iteration 9 = -8.169538E+003
The value of the likelihood function at iteration 10 = -8.169538E+003
The value of the likelihood function at iteration 11 = -8.169532E+003
The value of the likelihood function at iteration 12 = -8.169532E+003

Iterations stopped due to small change in likelihood function

******* ITERATION 13 *******

Sigma—squared =   0.30078   *Final estimate of the level-1 variance*

Standard Error of Sigma—squared =   0.00506

```
Tau(pi)
   INTRCPT1,P0      0.64057        0.04683
       YEAR,P1      0.04683        0.01134
```
Final estimates of the level-2
variances and covariances

```
Standard Errors of Tau(pi)
   INTRCPT1,P0      0.02513        0.00498
       YEAR,P1      0.00498        0.00190

Tau(pi) (as correlations)
   INTRCPT1,P0  1.000  0.550
       YEAR,P1  0.550  1.000
```
Note that the correlation between true
status at Year 3.5 (half way through third
grade) and true rate of change is estimated
to be 0.550 for children in the same school.

```
----------------------------------------------------
  Random level-1 coefficient   Reliability estimate
----------------------------------------------------
  INTRCPT1, P0                       0.840
      YEAR, P1                       0.192
```
Reliabilities of child
parameter estimates

```
Tau(beta)
  INTRCPT1        YEAR
  INTRCPT2,B00 INTRCPT2,B10
    0.16535        0.01700
    0.01700        0.01104
```
Final estimates of the level-3 variances and covariances.

```
Tau(beta) (as correlations)
  INTRCPT1/INTRCPT2,B00  1.000  0.398
      YEAR/INTRCPT2,B10  0.398  1.000
```
Notice that the correlation between true school mean status at Year 3.5 and true school-mean rate of change is 0.398.

```
Standard Errors of Tau(beta)
  INTRCPT1        YEAR
  INTRCPT2,B00 INTRCPT2,B10
    0.03642        0.00720
    0.00720        0.00252
```

```
-------------------------------------------------------
Random level-2 coefficient   Reliability estimate
-------------------------------------------------------

INTRCPT1/INTRCPT2, B00                 0.821
    YEAR/INTRCPT2, B10                 0.786
```
Reliabilities of school-level parameter estimates.

The value of the likelihood function at iteration 13 = -8.169532E+003

The outcome variable is   MATH

Final estimation of fixed effects:

Fixed Effect	Coefficient	Standard Error	T-ratio	P-value
For INTRCPT1, P0				
For INTRCPT2, B00				
INTRCPT3, G000	-0.779373	0.057834	-13.476	0.000
For YEAR slope, P1				
For INTRCPT2, B10				
INTRCPT3, G100	0.763259	0.015272	49.977	0.000

The above table indicates that the average growth rate is significantly positive at 0.763 logits per year, $t = 49.98$.

Final estimation of level-1 and level-2 variance components:

Random Effect		Standard Deviation	Variance Component	df	Chi-square	P-value
INTRCPT1,	R0	0.80036	0.64057	1661	6051.75707	0.000
YEAR slope,	R1	0.10648	0.01134	1661	2088.72049	0.000
level-1,	E	0.54843	0.30078			

The results above indicate significant variability among children within the same school in terms of status at Year 3.5 (chi-square = 6051.76) and in terms of rates of change (chi-square of 2088.72).

Final estimation of level-3 variance components:

Random Effect	Standard Deviation	Variance Component	df	Chi-square	P-value
INTRCPT1/INTRCPT2, U0	0.40663	0.16535	59	488.51571	0.000
YEAR/INTRCPT2, U1	0.10507	0.01104	59	377.78011	0.000

The results above indicate significant variability among schools in terms of mean status at Year 3.5 (chi-square = 488.52) and in terms of school-mean rates of change (chi-square of 377.78).

Statistics for current covariance components model

```
Deviance                      = 16339.063067
Number of estimated parameters = 9
```

Exploratory Analysis: estimated level-2 coefficients and their standard errors
        obtained by regressing EB residuals on level-2 predictors selected for
        possible inclusion in subsequent HLM runs

Level-1 Coefficient	Potential Level-2 Predictors		
	GENDER	BLACK	HISPANIC
INTRCPT1, P0			
Coefficient	-0.011	-0.362	-0.032
Standard Error	0.036	0.067	0.070
t value	-0.311	-5.432	-0.463
	GENDER	BLACK	HISPANIC
YEAR, P1			
Coefficient	0.001	-0.029	0.005
Standard Error	0.003	0.006	0.006
t value	0.361	-4.830	0.795

Exploratory Analysis: estimated level-3 coefficients and their standard errors
        obtained by regressing EB residuals on level-3 predictors selected for
        possible inclusion in subsequent HLM runs

Level-2 Predictor	Potential Level-3 Predictors		
	SIZE	LOWINC	MOBILE
INTRCPT1/INTRCPT2, B00			
Coefficient	0.000	-0.009	-0.016
Standard Error	0.000	0.002	0.004
t value	-1.650	-5.099	-4.323

```
                       SIZE    LOWINC   MOBILE
       YEAR/INTRCPT2, B10
       Coefficient     0.000   -0.001   -0.002
       Standard Error  0.000    0.000    0.001
       t value        -1.520   -2.872   -1.946
```

Just as in the case of the two-level program, the potential of predictors not included in the model to be employed as significant predictors in subsequent models is indicated approximately by the "t-values" given above. Note, because of the metric of school size (100s and 1000s), the actual coefficients and standard errors are too small to be printed. The t-values are not, however.

Model checking based on the residual files

HLM/3L produces two residual files, one at level-2 (containing estimates of the π's) and one at level-3 (containing estimates of the β's). These files will contain the EB residuals defined at levels 2 and 3, fitted values, and OL residuals. By adding the EB residuals to the corresponding fitted values, the analyst can also obtain the EB estimate for the corresponding coefficients. In addition, level-2 predictors can be included in the level-2 residual file and level-3 predictors in the level-3 residual file. However, other statistics provided in the residual file of HLM/2L (*e.g.*, the Mahalanobis distance measures) are not available in the residual files produced by HLM/3L.

An example of a level-2 residual file produced in the above analysis is illustrated below. Only the data from the first and last pairs of children are given.

The files in this example are structured as SYSTAT command files and can be directly read into that program to create SYSTAT system files. As with HLM/2L, the user can also specify SAS or SPSS command file format for the residual file. The result will be executable SAS or SPSS programs. (For more details see section *Model checking based on the residual file* on page 11.) Alternatively, the data defining information at the top of the file can be used to read these residual files into an alternative computing package.

We see that the level-3 id (*group id* or *GID*) is the first variable and the level-2 id (*person id* or *PID*) is the second. Each is written in an alphanumeric format (note the "$" indicator) and takes 10 columns. The rest of the variables are numeric and include *NJK*, the number of observations associated with child j in school k. Next come the empirical Bayes estimates of the residuals, r_{pjk}, including, respectively, the intercept (*EBINTRCP*) and the *year* effect (*EBYEAR*); then the ordinary least squares estimates of the same quantities (*OLINTRCP* and *OLYEAR*); and finally, the fitted values, that is, the predicted values of the π_{pjk}'s for a given child based on the fixed effects (*FVINTRCP* and *FVYEAR*) and random school effect.

```
SAVE RESFIL2
LRECL=255
INPUT (GID$,PID$,NJK,
EBINTRCP,EBYEAR   ,
OLINTRCP,OLYEAR   ,
FVINTRCP,FVYEAR   ,
),($12,$12,#5/ 2*#11/ 2*#11/ 2*#11)
if OLINTRCP=-99 then let OLINTRCP=.
if OLYEAR  =-99 then let OLYEAR  =.
RUN
       2020    273026452 3
      0.2451       0.0040
      0.8666      -0.3762
     -0.2054       0.9532
       2020    273030991 5
      1.1232       0.1242
      1.1357       0.2635
     -0.2054       0.9532
     .  .  .

     .  .  .
       4450    310621871 3
     -0.6639      -0.0377
     -0.7178       0.0823
     -0.9637       0.6507
       4450    314542551 3
      0.1849      -0.0248
     -0.0901      -0.7037
     -0.9637       0.6507
```

We see, then, that the first child in the data set has *school id* 2020 and *child id* 273026452. That child has 3 time-series observations. The predicted growth rate for that child (the *Year* effect) is the fitted value .9532. That child's empirical Bayes residual *year* effect is .0040. Thus, the investigator can construct the empirical Bayes estimate of that child's *year* effect as:

$$\pi^*_{1jk} = \beta^*_{10k} + r^*_{1jk}$$
$$= FVYEAR + EBYEAR$$
$$= .9532 + .0040 = .9572 .$$

In a similar fashion, the investigator can also compute the empirical Bayes estimate for the child's intercept, π^*_{0jk}, using $FVINTRCP + EBINTRCP$.

The level-3 residual file, printed below, has a similar structure. Only the data from the first and last schools are given. We see that the level-3 id (*group id* or *GID*) is the first variable and is written in alphanumeric format (note the "$" indicator) and takes 12 columns. The rest of the variables are numeric and include *NK*, the number of children in school k. Next come the empirical Bayes estimates of the β's, including, respectively, the intercept (*EB00*) and the *year* effect (*EB10*); then, the ordinary least squares estimates of the same quantities (*OL00* and *OL10*); and finally, the fitted values, that is, the predicted values of the β's for a given school based on that school's effect and the fixed effects (*FV00* and *FV01*).

```
SAVE RESFIL3
LRECL=255
INPUT (GID$,NK,
EB00,EB10,
OL00,OL10,
FV00,FV01,
),($12,#5/ 2*#11/ 2*#11/ 2*#11)
if OL00=-99 then let OL00=.
if OL10=-99 then let OL10=.
RUN
        2020 21
     0.5739      0.1899
     0.6361      0.1975
    -0.7794      0.7633
       .  .  .

       .  .  .
        4450 45
    -0.1843     -0.1126
    -0.2341     -0.1893
    -0.7794      0.7633
```

We see, then, that the first unit, school 2020, has $NK = 21$ children. The predicted *year* effect for school 2020 is the fitted value .7633, that is, the maximum-likelihood estimate of the school mean growth rate in the case of this unconditional model. That school's empirical Bayes residual *year* effect is .1899. Thus, the investigator can construct the empirical Bayes estimate of that school's *year* effect (mean rate of growth) as

$$
\begin{aligned}
\beta_{10k}^{*} &= \gamma_{100}^{*} + u_{1k}^{*} \\
&= FV01 + EB10 \\
&= .7633 + .1899 = .9532 \ .
\end{aligned}
$$

Similarly, the investigator can construct the empirical Bayes estimate for the school's intercept, β_{00k}^{*}, using *FV00 + EB00*.

Note that the empirical Bayes estimate of the school *year* effect, 0.9532, is the fitted value for each child in that school (in the level-2 residual file). This will be true in any model that is unconditional at level 2, that is, any model with no child-level predictors such as *race/ethnicity* or *gender*. When level-2 predictors are in the model, the level-2 fitted values will also depend on those predictors.

Using HLM/3L in batch mode

Constructing the SSM file using an "RSP" file

When the user constructs an SSM file interactively, HLM/3L automatically creates a file named CREATESS.RSP that lists the stream of responses typed by the user. The CREATESS.RSP file for the HLM/3L session illustrated in the section *Constructing the SSM file from raw data* on page 84 is listed below:

```
Y
1
4
(A4,1X,A9,1X,2F5.1,F7.3,F2.0)
EG1.DAT
3
(A4,1X,A9,3F2.0)
EG2.DAT
3
(A4,1X,3F7.1)
EG3.DAT
```

```
       YEAR
      GRADE
       MATH
   RETAINED
     GENDER
      BLACK
   HISPANIC
       SIZE
     LOWINC
     MOBILE
N
N
EG.SSM
Y
```

The CREATESS.RSP file has several uses. It can help the user discover errors in the format or variable name specification. Once these are identified, CREATESS.RSP can be copied, for example, to NEWSS.RSP, and then edited. Alternatively, if the user wishes to delete or add variables, the copy of CREATESS.RSP can be edited. To reconstruct the SSM file using this new set of commands, simply type:

```
HLM3L -R NEWSS.RSP
```

Executing analyses based on the SSM file

As in the case of HLM/2L, formulation, estimation, and testing of models using HLM/3L can be achieved in several ways: Windows mode (PC users only), interactive mode, or batch mode. HLM/3L for Windows closely parallels HLM/2L for Windows. For further information about the Windows implementation, see the "Help" facility within the HLM/3L for Windows program.

Interactive execution guides the user through the steps of the analysis by posing questions and providing a menu of options. However, batch mode can be considerably faster once the user becomes skilled in working with the program. In between the two extremes — fully interactive and fully batch — is a range of execution modes that are partly interactive and partly batch. The degree to which the user automates execution via batch mode is controlled by the command file, as in the case of HLM/2L.

Command file keywords

The command file structure for HLM/3L closely parallels that of HLM/2L. Each line begins with a keyword followed by a colon. After the colon is the option chosen by the user, *i.e.*,

```
keyword:option
```

As with HLM/2L a "#" as the first character of a line can be used to introduce a comment into the command file.

The following keywords have the same definitions and options in HLM/3L as in HLM/2L (Section *Table of Keywords and Options* on page 42):

> `numit, constrain, hypoth, gamma#, deviance, df, title, output, stopval, accel, macroit, microit, stopmacro, stopmicro, sigma2, nonlin,` and `resfiltype`.

The following keywords are available only for HLM/2L:

> `lev1ols, homvar, mlf,` and `plausvals`.

The basic HLM/3L command file

A basic command file will be used by HLM/3L by default, that is, unless the user specifies an alternative. This default command file specifies: use of the "standard" computer generated starting values (`fixtau2:3` and `fixtau3:3`) for the variance and covariances; no optional hypothesis testing (`hypoth:n`); and that the user is not interested in constraining the level-3 coefficients (`constrain:n`). It also sets the default stopping value for testing convergence of maximum-likelihood estimates. These specifications are set in a file named `COMFILE3.HLM` that comes with the HLM/3L program:

```
fixtau2:3
fixtau3:3
constrain:n
```

Table 4.1

Keywords and options unique to the HLM/3L command file

Keyword	Function	Option	Definition
level1	Level-1 model specification	intrcpt1	Level-1 intercept
		varname	Level-1 predictor (no centering)
		varname,1	Level-1 predictor centered around unit mean $a_{.jk}$
		varname,2	Level-1 predictor centered around grand mean $a_{...}$
	(Note: variable names may be specified in either upper or lower case)		
level2	Level-2 model specification	intrcpt2	Level-2 intercept
		varname	Level-2 predictor (no centering)
		varname,1	Level-2 predictor centered around group mean, $X_{.k}$
		varname,2	Level-2 predictor centered around grand mean, $X_{..}$
		/*varlist*	List after the slash level-2 variables for exploratory analysis and "t-to-enter statistics" on subsequent runs. A slash without a subsequent variable list suppresses the interactive prompt.
level3	Level-3 model specification	intrcpt3	Level-3 intercept (must be included in the level-2 model)
		varname	Level-3 predictor (no centering)
		varname,2	Level-3 predictor centered around grand mean $W_{.}$
		/*varlist*	List after the slash level-3 variables for exploratory analysis and "t-to-enter statistics" on subsequent runs. A slash without a subsequent variable list suppresses the interactive prompt.

Continues

Table 4.1 (continued)

Keywords and options unique to the HLM/3L command file

Keyword	Function	Option	Definition
resfil2	Create a residual file at level 2	y/*varlist*	Yes, create. The *varlist* after the slash is optional. The user may include other potential level-2 predictors in the residual file.
		n	No, do not save.
resfil2name	Name of residual file	*filename*	Changes the default (resfil2.cmd).
resfil3	Create a residual file at level 3	y/*varlist*	Yes, create. The *varlist* after the slash is optional. The user may include other potential level-3 predictors in the residual file.
		n	No, do not save.
resfil3name	Name of residual file	*filename*	Changes the default (resfil3.cmd).
fixtau2	Method of correcting unacceptable starting values for T_π	1	Set all off-diagonal elements to 0.
		2	Manually reset starting values.
		3	Automatic fix-up.
		4	Terminate run.
		5	Stop program after computing starting values even if acceptable; display starting values and then allow user to manually reset them.
fixtau3	Method of correcting unacceptable starting values for T_β	1	Set all off-diagonal elements to 0.
		2	Manually reset starting values.
		3	Automatic fix-up.
		4	Terminate run.
		5	Stop program after computing starting values even if acceptable; display starting values and then allow user to manually reset them.

HLM/3L uses COMFILE3.HLM by default. (This file is kept in a system-dependent location. Under DOS, it is usually in c:\HLM.) However, this can be overridden by specifying a third parameter on the command line when starting the program:

HLM3L *ssmfile comfile*

where *ssmfile* is the name of the SSM file that provides the data and *comfile* is the customized command file that the user wishes to use as a substitute for COMFILE3.HLM. Note that both *ssmfile* and *comfile* should be specified with the correct drive and directory if these files are not in the working directory.

Model specification via a command file

The command file, COMFILE3.HLM, supplies no information about the variable to be included in the analysis. To run HLM/3L in batch mode, the user specifies the variables for the analysis much as in the case of HLM/2L (see Section *Some Examples of Model Specification via a Command File* on page 48 for a detailed discussion). The command file below replicates the results of the interactive session presented above (see section *Example: constructing an SSM file for the urban public school data* on page 88):

```
level1:math=intrcpt1+year+random/
level2:intrcpt1=intrcpt2+random/gender,black,hispanic
level3:intrcpt2=intrcpt3+random/size,lowinc,mobile
level2:year=intrcpt2+random/gender,black,hispanic
level3:intrcpt2=intrcpt3+random/size,lowinc,mobile
numit:200
hypoth:n
stopval:.000001
constrain:n
fixtau2:3
fixtau3:3
resfil2:n
resfil3:n
output:eg1.lis
title:Unconditional Linear Growth Model
nonlin:n
accel:5
```

We examine the model specification (first five lines) in more detail.

□ The first line specifies the level-1 model. Thus

`level1:math=intrcpt1+year+random`

is equivalent to the equation

$$Y_{ijk} = \pi_{0jk} + \pi_{1jk}(year)_{ijk} + e_{ijk} ,$$

where Y_{ijk} is the *math* outcome score at time i for child j in school k. This model specifies two growth coefficients, π_{0jk} and π_{1jk}, for each child.

□ The next two lines in the command file specify the level-2 and level-3 models for π_{0jk}. We have

`level2:intrcpt1=intrcpt2+random/gender,black,hispanic`

which is equivalent to

$$\pi_{0jk} = \beta_{00k} + r_{0jk} ,$$

and

`level3:intrcpt2=intrcpt3+random/size,lowinc,mobile`

which is equivalent to

$$\beta_{00k} = \gamma_{000} + u_{00k} .$$

The variable lists after the forward slash (/) identify variables at levels 2 and 3, respectively, to be included in the "exploratory analysis" for other potential predictors at each level.

□ The following pair of lines specify the level-2 and level-3 models for π_{1jk}. We have:

`level2:year=intrcpt2+random/gender,black,hispanic`
`level3:intrcpt2=intrcpt3+random/size,lowinc,mobile`

These lines are equivalent to

$$\pi_{1jk} = \beta_{10k} + r_{1jk} ,$$

and

$$\beta_{10k} = \gamma_{100} + u_{10k} .$$

The representation in the HLM/3L output for this model is:

```
Level-1 Model

    Y = P0 + P1*(year) + E

Level-2 Model

    P0 = B00 + R0
    P1 = B10 + R1

Level-3 Model

    B00 = G000 + U0
    B10 = G100 + U1
```

This example involves a model that is "unconditional" at levels 2 and 3; that is, no predictors are specified at each of those levels. Such a model is useful for partitioning variation in intercepts and growth rates into components that lie within and between schools (see *Hierarchical Linear Models*, Chapter 8), but provides no information on how child or school characteristics relate to the growth curves. The command file below models the intercept and growth rates as functions of race/ethnicity at level 2. At level 3, we incorporate information about a school's percent low income into the model. Moreover, we explore the possibility that several other predictors (gender, school enrollment, and percent mobility) might help account for variation in subsequent models:

```
level1:math=intrcpt1+year+random/
level2:intrcpt1=intrcpt2+black+hispanic+random/gender
level3:intrcpt2=intrcpt3+lowinc+random/size,mobile
level3:black=intrcpt3/
level3:hispanic=intrcpt3/
level2:year=intrcpt2+black+hispanic+random/gender
level3:intrcpt2=intrcpt3+lowinc+random/size,mobile
level3:black=intrcpt3/
level3:hispanic=intrcpt3/
nonlin:n
numit:200
fixtau2:3
fixtau3:3
fixsigma2:n
stopval:.000001
constrain:n
hypoth:n
resfil2:n
resfil3:n
title:Linear growth over grade, minority, low income
output:eg3.lis
```

Note that the level-1 model (the first line) has remained unchanged. However, the level-2 and level-3 models for π_{0jk} have been elaborated so that the next four lines

```
level2:intrcpt1=intrcpt2+black+hispanic+random/gender
level3:intrcpt2=intrcpt3+lowinc+random/size,mobile
level3:black=intrcpt3/
level3:hispanic=intrcpt3/
```

are equivalent to

$$\pi_{0jk} = \beta_{00k} + \beta_{01k}(Black)_{jk} + \beta_{02k}(Hispanic)_{jk} + r_{0jk},$$
$$\beta_{00k} = \gamma_{000} + \gamma_{001}(lowinc)_k + u_{00k},$$
$$\beta_{01k} = \gamma_{010}, \quad \text{and}$$
$$\beta_{02k} = \gamma_{020}.$$

The first of these four equations tells us that a child's intercept (recall, this is the predicted math achievement of that child at 3.5 years) depends on race/ethnicity as indicated by *Black, Hispanic,* or other. The inclusion of /gender in the corresponding command file line tells HLM/3L to include *gender* in the "exploratory analysis" for other potential level-2 predictors. The second equation says that the school-specific intercept (which is now the predicted mean achievement for white students in school k) depends on the percent of low income students in the school. School enrollment and percent mobility will be checked for their usefulness in subsequent models (via the symbols /size,mobile). The third and fourth equations tell us that the effects associated with race/ethnicity are assumed invariant across schools (*i.e.,* "fixed").

A parallel set of four equations specify the level-2 and level-3 model for growth rates, π_{1jk}. Thus, corresponding to the lines

```
level2:year=intrcpt2+black+hispanic+random/gender
level3:intrcpt2=intrcpt3+lowinc+random/size,mobile
level3:black=intrcpt3/
level3:hispanic=intrcpt3/
```

are the four equations

$$\pi_{1jk} = \beta_{10k} + \beta_{11k}(Black)_{jk} + \beta_{12k}(Hispanic)_{jk} + r_{1k},$$
$$\beta_{10k} = \gamma_{100} + \gamma_{101}(lowinc)_k + u_{10k},$$
$$\beta_{11k} = \gamma_{110}, \quad \text{and}$$
$$\beta_{12k} = \gamma_{120}.$$

Note, the order of equations in the command file is important. The level-1 equation must come first, followed by the complete modeling at levels 2 and 3 for intrcpt1. *This is then followed by the complete modeling at levels 2 and 3 for the first level-1 coefficient (for "year") and then for any subsequent level-1 coefficients. This nested specification order must be followed.*

The results of this analysis are given below.

```
****************************************************************
*                                                              *
*       HH    HH  LL        MM    MM    333                     *
*       HH    HH  LL        MMM  MMM   33333                    *
*       HH    HH  LL        MMMM MMMM 33   33                   *
*       HHHHHHHH  LL        MM MMM MM      33                   *
*       HHHHHHHH  LL        MM  M  MM      33                   *
*       HH    HH  LL        MM    MM   33   33                  *
*       HH    HH  LLLLLLLL  MM    MM   33333                    *
*       HH    HH  LLLLLLLL  MM    MM    333                     *
*                   Version 4.01                               *
****************************************************************

SPECIFICATIONS FOR THIS HLM RUN                 Mon Feb  5 14:18:22 1996
-------------------------------------------------------------------------------

Problem Title: Linear growth over grade, minority, low income

The data source for this run = eg.ssm
Output file name            = eg3.lis
The maximum number of level-2 units = 1721
The maximum number of level-3 units = 60
The maximum number of iterations = 200
Method of estimation: full maximum likelihood

The outcome variable is     MATH

The model specified for the fixed effects was:
-----------------------------------------------------

Level-1              Level-2           Level-3
Coefficients         Predictors        Predictors
--------------------  ----------------  ----------------
    INTRCPT1, P0         INTRCPT2, B00     INTRCPT3, G000
                                           LOWINC, G001
                     #     BLACK, B01     INTRCPT3, G010
                     # HISPANIC, B02     INTRCPT3, G020
    YEAR slope, P1       INTRCPT2, B10     INTRCPT3, G100
                                           LOWINC, G101
                     #     BLACK, B11     INTRCPT3, G110
                     # HISPANIC, B12     INTRCPT3, G120

'#' - The residual parameter variance for the parameter has been set to zero
```

Summary of the model specified (in equation format)

Level-1 Model

     Y = P0 + P1*(YEAR) + E

Level-2 Model

     P0 = B00 + B01*(BLACK) + B02*(HISPANIC) + R0
     P1 = B10 + B11*(BLACK) + B12*(HISPANIC) + R1

Level-3 Model

     B00 = G000 + G001(LOWINC) + U0
     B01 = G010
     B02 = G020
     B10 = G100 + G101(LOWINC) + U1
     B11 = G110
     B12 = G120

For starting values, data from 7242 level-1 and 1721 level-2 records were used

STARTING VALUES

Sigma—squared(0) =   0.29630

Tau(pi)(0)
 INTRCPT1,P0   0.69346   0.04904
     YEAR,P1   0.04904   0.01507

Tau(beta)(0)
 INTRCPT1   YEAR
 INTRCPT2,B00 INTRCPT2,B10
    0.05929   0.00283
    0.00283   0.01057

The value of the likelihood function at iteration 1 = -8.133928E+003
The value of the likelihood function at iteration 2 = -8.128381E+003
The value of the likelihood function at iteration 3 = -8.127723E+003
The value of the likelihood function at iteration 4 = -8.127499E+003
The value of the likelihood function at iteration 5 = -8.127367E+003

                                                .
                                              .
                                              .

The value of the likelihood function at iteration 9 = -8.125892E+003
The value of the likelihood function at iteration 10 = -8.125892E+003
The value of the likelihood function at iteration 11 = -8.125886E+003
The value of the likelihood function at iteration 12 = -8.125886E+003

Iterations stopped due to small change in likelihood function

                                                          4 WORKING WITH HLM/3L

```
******* ITERATION 13 *******


Sigma-squared =        0.30093

Standard Error of Sigma-squared =        0.00509


Tau(pi)
  INTRCPT1,P0      0.62237      0.04667
       YEAR,P1      0.04667      0.01117

Standard Errors of Tau(pi)
  INTRCPT1,P0      0.02449      0.00491
       YEAR,P1      0.00491      0.00189

Tau(pi) (as correlations)
  INTRCPT1,P0   1.000   0.560
       YEAR,P1   0.560   1.000


------------------------------------------------
Random level-1 coefficient   Reliability estimate
------------------------------------------------
  INTRCPT1, P0                     0.836
       YEAR, P1                     0.189


Tau(beta)
  INTRCPT1          YEAR
  INTRCPT2,B00  INTRCPT2,B10
     0.07814       0.00075
     0.00075       0.00799

Tau(beta) (as correlations)
  INTRCPT1/INTRCPT2,B00   1.000   0.030
       YEAR/INTRCPT2,B10   0.030   1.000

Standard Errors of Tau(beta)
  INTRCPT1          YEAR
  INTRCPT2,B00  INTRCPT2,B10
     0.01992       0.00441
     0.00441       0.00194


------------------------------------------------
Random level-2 coefficient   Reliability estimate
------------------------------------------------
  INTRCPT1/INTRCPT2, B00              0.702
       YEAR/INTRCPT2, B10              0.735

The value of the likelihood function at iteration 13 = -8.125886E+003
```

The outcome variable is   MATH

Final estimations of fixed effects:

    Fixed Effect   Coefficient   Standard Error   T-ratio   P-value
----
For   INTRCPT1, P0
   For INTRCPT2, B00
      INTRCPT3, G000   0.140589   0.127515   1.103   0.275
         LOWINC, G001   -0.007577   0.001691   -4.481   0.000
      For   BLACK, B01
      INTRCPT3, G010   -0.502222   0.077874   -6.449   0.000
   For HISPANIC, B02
      INTRCPT3, G020   -0.319557   0.086081   -3.712   0.000
For   YEAR slope, P1
   For INTRCPT2, B10
      INTRCPT3, G100   0.874802   0.039158   22.340   0.000
         LOWINC, G101   -0.001374   0.000523   -2.628   0.007
      For   BLACK, B11
      INTRCPT3, G110   -0.030717   0.022458   -1.368   0.171
   For HISPANIC, B12
      INTRCPT3, G120   0.043934   0.024646   1.783   0.074

Final estimation of level-1 and level-2 variance components:

Random Effect   Standard   Variance   df   Chi-square P-value
                         Deviation   Component

INTRCPT1,   R0   0.78890   0.62237   1659   7992.93790   0.000
   YEAR slope,   R1   0.10567   0.01117   1659   2095.63565   0.000
  level-1,   E   0.54857   0.30093

Final estimation of level-3 variance components:

Random Effect   Standard   Variance   df   Chi-square P-value
                         Deviation   Component

INTRCPT1/INTRCPT2, U0   0.27953   0.07814   58   255.18231   0.000
      YEAR/INTRCPT2, U1   0.08939   0.00799   58   277.43657   0.000

Statistics for current covariance components model

Deviance   = 16251.772372
Number of estimated parameters = 15

```
Exploratory Analysis: estimated level-2 coefficients and their standard errors
                obtained by regressing EB residuals on level-2 predictors selected for
                possible inclusion in subsequent HLM runs
----------------------------------------------------------------------------
Level-1 Coefficient              Potential Level-2 Predictors
----------------------------------------------------------------------------


                                 GENDER
INTRCPT1, P0
    Coefficient                  -0.010
    Standard Error                0.036
    t value                      -0.272


                                 GENDER
    YEAR, P1
    Coefficient                   0.001
    Standard Error                0.003
    t value                       0.447



Exploratory Analysis: estimated level-3 coefficients and their standard errors
                obtained by regressing EB residuals on level-3 predictors selected for
                possible inclusion in subsequent HLM runs
----------------------------------------------------------------------------
Level-2 Predictor                Potential Level-3 Predictors
----------------------------------------------------------------------------


                                 SIZE    MOBILE
INTRCPT1/INTRCPT2
    Coefficient                  0.000   -0.007
    Standard Error               0.000    0.002
    t value                     -0.715   -2.824


                                 SIZE    MOBILE
    YEAR/INTRCPT2
    Coefficient                  0.000    0.000
    Standard Error               0.000    0.001
    t value                     -1.152   -0.522
```

Other program features

Like HLM/2L, HLM/3L provides options for multivariate hypothesis tests for
the fixed effects and the variance-covariance components. A "no-intercept" model is available at level 1 or level 2 (but not at level 3). Missing
data options are available at level 1 (but not at levels 2 or 3). Options
available on HLM/2L but not HLM/3L include the preliminary exploratory

analysis option, the test of homogeneity of variance at level 1, the specification of a random effect having no corresponding fixed effect, and plausible value averaging.

5

Conceptual and Statistical Background for Hierarchical Generalized Linear Models (HGLM)

The hierarchical linear model (HLM) as described in the previous four chapters is appropriate for two- and three-level data where the random effects at each level are normally distributed. The assumption of normality at level-1 is quite widely applicable when the outcome variable is continuous. Even when a continuous outcome is highly skewed, a transformation can often be found that will make the distribution of level-1 random effects (residuals) at least roughly normal. Methods for assessing the normality of random effects at higher levels are discussed on page 32 above and on page 218 of *Hierarchical Linear Models*.

There are important cases, however, where the assumption of normality at level-1 is clearly not realistic and no transformation can make it so. An example is a binary outcome, Y, indicating the presence of a disease ($Y = 1$ if the disease is present, $Y = 0$ if the disease is absent), graduation from high school ($Y = 1$ if a student graduates on time, $Y = 0$ if not), or the commission of a crime ($Y = 1$ if a person commits a crime during given time interval, $Y = 0$ if not). The use of the standard level-1 model in this case would be inappropriate for three reasons:

- ❏ Given the predicted value of the outcome, the level-1 random effect can only take on one of two values, and therefore cannot be normally distributed;
- ❏ The level-1 random effect cannot have homogeneous variance. Instead, the variance of this random effect depends on the predicted value as specified below.

☐ Finally, there are no restrictions on the predicted values of the level-1 outcome in the standard HLM: they can legitimately take on any real value. In contrast, the predicted value of a binary outcome Y, if viewed as the predicted probability that $Y = 1$, cannot meaningfully be less than zero or greater than unity. Thus, an appropriate model for predicting Y ought to constrain the predicted values to lie in the interval $(0, 1)$. This constraint will give meaning to the effect sizes estimated by the model.

Another example, not appropriately analyzed using the standard HLM involves count data, for example where Y is the number of crimes a person commits during a year or Y is the number of questions a child asks during the course of a one-hour class period. In these cases, the possible values of Y are non-negative integers $0, 1, 2, \ldots$ Such data will typically be positively skewed. If there are very few zeros in the data, a transformation, *e.g.*, $Y^\star = \log(1 + Y)$, may solve this problem and allow sensible use of the standard HLM. However, in the cases mentioned above, there will typically be many zeros (many persons will not commit a crime during a given year and many children will not raise a question during a one-hour class). When there are many zeros, the normality assumption cannot be approximated by a transformation. Also, as in the case of the binary outcome, the variance of the level-1 random effects will depend on the predicted value (higher predicted values will have larger variance). Similarly, the predicted values ought to be constrained to be positive.

Within HLM, the user can specify a nonlinear analysis appropriate for binary and count data. The approach is a direct extension of the generalized linear model of McCullagh & Nelder (1989) to the case of hierarchical data. We, therefore, refer to this approach as a "hierarchical generalized linear model" (HGLM). The execution of these analyses is in many ways similar to that in HLM but there are also important differences. The comparison between HLM and HGLM parallels a comparison of the standard linear regression model with the generalized linear model of McCullagh & Nelder (1989) in "single-level" models, though some new issues arise in moving to the multilevel setting.

The two-level HLM as a special case of HGLM

The level-1 model in the HGLM may be viewed as consisting of three parts: a sampling model, a link function, and a structural model. In fact, the standard HLM can be viewed as a special case of the HGLM where the sampling model is normal and the link function is the identity link.

Level-1 sampling model. The sampling model for a two-level HLM might be written as

$$Y_{ij}|\mu_{ij} \sim NID(\mu_{ij}, \sigma^2) , \qquad (5.1)$$

meaning that the level-one outcome Y_{ij}, given the predicted value, μ_{ij}, is normally and independently distributed with an expected value of μ_{ij} and a constant variance, σ^2. The level-1 expected value and mean may alternatively be written as

$$E(Y_{ij}|\mu_{ij}) = \mu_{ij} \qquad Var(Y_{ij}|\mu_{ij}) = \sigma^2 . \qquad (5.2)$$

Level-1 link function. In general it is possible to transform the level-1 predicted value, μ_{ij}, to η_{ij} to insure that the predictions are constrained to lie within a given interval. Such a transformation is called a link function. In the normal case, no transformation is necessary. However, this decision not to transform may be made explicit by writing

$$\eta_{ij} = \mu_{ij} . \qquad (5.3)$$

The link function in this case is viewed as the "identity link function."

Level-1 structural model. The transformed predicted value is now related to the predictors of the model through the linear model or "structural model"

$$\eta_{ij} = \beta_{0j} + \beta_{1j}X_{1ij} + \beta_{2j}X_{2ij} + \cdots + \beta_{Qj}X_{Qij} . \qquad (5.4)$$

It is clear that, combining the level-1 sampling model (5.1), the level-1 link function (5.3), and the level-1 structural model (5.4) reproduces the level-1 model of HLM (1.1). In the context of a standard HLM, it seems silly to write three equations where only one is needed, but the value of the extra equations becomes apparent in the case of binary and count data.

Two- and three-level models for binary outcomes

While the standard HLM uses a normal sampling model and an identity link function, the binary outcome model uses a binomial sampling model and a logit link.

Level-1 sampling model. Let Y_{ij} be the number of "successes" in n_{ij} trials. Then we write that

$$Y_{ij}|\phi_{ij} \sim B(n_{ij}, \phi_{ij}) , \tag{5.5}$$

to denote that Y_{ij} has a binomial distribution with n_{ij} trials and probability of success ϕ_{ij}. According to the binomial distribution, the expected value and variance of Y_{ij} are then

$$E(Y_{ij}|\phi_{ij}) = n_{ij}\phi_{ij} \qquad Var(Y_{ij}|\phi_{ij}) = n_{ij}\phi_{ij}(1 - \phi_{ij}) . \tag{5.6}$$

When $n_{ij} = 1$, Y_{ij} may take on values of either zero or unity. This is a special case of the binomial distribution known as the Bernoulli distribution. HGLM allows estimation of models in which $n_{ij} = 1$ (Bernoulli case) or $n_{ij} > 1$ (other binomial cases). The case with $n_{ij} > 1$ will be treated later.

For the Bernoulli case, the predicted value of the binary Y_{ij} is equal to the probability of a success, ϕ_{ij}. Thus, for this HGLM application $\mu_{ij} = \phi_{ij}$.

Level-1 link function. When the level-1 sampling model is binomial, HGLM uses the logit link function

$$\eta_{ij} = \log\left(\frac{\mu_{ij}}{1 - \mu_{ij}}\right). \tag{5.7}$$

In words, η_{ij} is the log of the odds of success. Thus if the probability of success, μ_{ij}, is 0.5, the odds of success is 1.0 and the log-odds or "logit" is zero. When the probability of success is less than 0.5, the odds are less than one and the logit is negative; when the probability is greater than 0.5, the odds are greater than unity and the logit is positive. Thus, while μ_{ij} is constrained to be in the interval $(0, 1)$, η_{ij} can take on any real value.

Level-1 structural model. This will have exactly the same form as (5.4). Note that estimates of the β's in (5.4) make it possible to generate a predicted log-odds (η_{ij}) for any case. Such a predicted log-odds can be converted to an odds by computing *odds = exponential*(η_{ij}). Similarly, predicted log-odds can be converted to a *predicted probability* by computing

$$\mu_{ij} = \frac{1}{1 + \exp(-\eta_{ij})}, \tag{5.8}$$

Clearly, whatever the value of η_{ij}, applying (5.8) will produce a μ_{ij} between zero and unity.

Level-2 and Level-3 models. In the case of a two-level analysis, the level-2 model has the same form as used in a standard 2-level HLM (equations 1.2, 1.3, and 1.4). In the case of a three-level analysis, the level-2 and level-3 models are also the same as in a standard 3-level HLM.

The model for count data

For count data, we use a Poisson sampling model and a log link function.

Level-1 sampling model. Let Y_{ij} be the number of events occurring during an interval time having length n_{ij}. For example, Y_{ij} could be the number of crimes a person i in group j commits during five years, so that $n_{ij} = 5$. The time-interval of n_{ij} units may be termed the "exposure." Then we write that

$$Y_{ij}|\lambda_{ij} \sim P(n_{ij}, \lambda_{ij}) \qquad (5.9)$$

to denote that Y_{ij} has a Poisson distribution with exposure n_{ij} and event rate λ_{ij}. According to the Poisson distribution, the expected value and variance of Y_{ij} are then

$$E(Y_{ij}|\lambda_{ij}) = n_{ij}\lambda_{ij} \qquad Var(Y_{ij}|\lambda_{ij}) = n_{ij}\lambda_{ij} \ . \qquad (5.10)$$

The exposure n_{ij} need not be a measure of time. For example, if Y_{ij} is the number of bombs dropping on neighborhood i of city j during a war, n_{ij} could be the area of that neighborhood. A common case arises when for every i and j the exposure is the same (*e.g.*, Y_{ij} is the number of crimes committed during one year for each person i within each neighborhood j). In this case, we set $n_{ij} = 1$ for simplicity. HGLM allows estimation of models in which $n_{ij} = 1$ or $n_{ij} > 1$. (The case with $n_{ij} > 1$ will be treated later.)

According to our level-1 model, the predicted value of Y_{ij} when $n_{ij} = 1$, generically denoted μ_{ij}, will be the event rate λ_{ij}, so that, in this case $\mu_{ij} = \lambda_{ij}$.

Level-1 link function. HGLM uses the log link function when the level-1 sampling model is Poisson, that is

$$\eta_{ij} = \log(\mu_{ij}) \ , \qquad (5.11)$$

In words, η_{ij} is the log of the event rate. Thus, if the event rate, μ_{ij}, is one, the log is zero. When the event rate is less than one, the log is negative; when the event rate is greater than one, the log is positive. Thus, while μ_{ij} is constrained to be non-negative, η_{ij} can take on any real value.

Level-1 structural model. This will have exactly the same form as (5.4). Note that estimates of the β's in (5.4) make it possible to generate a predicted log-event rate (η_{ij}) for any case. Such a predicted log-event rate can be converted to an event rate by computing

$$\textit{event rate} = \textit{exponential}(\eta_{ij}) \ .$$

Clearly, whatever the value of η_{ij}, μ_{ij} will be non-negative.

Level-2 model. The level-2 model has the same form as the level-2 model for HLM/2L (equations 1.2, 1.3, and 1.4); and the level-2 and level-3 models have the same form in the three-level case as in HLM/3L.

Parameter estimation

HGLM bases inference on the joint posterior modes of the level-1 and level-2 (and level-3) regression coefficients given the variance-covariance estimates. The variance-covariance estimates are based on a normal approximation to the restricted likelihood. Stiratelli, Laird, & Ware (1984) and Wong & Mason (1985) developed this approach for the binary case. Schall (1991) discusses the extension of this approach to the wider class of generalized linear models. Breslow & Clayton (1993) refer to this estimation approach as "penalized quasi-likelihood" or PQL. Extending HLM to HGLM requires a doubly-iterative algorithm, significantly increasing computational time. Related approaches are described by Goldstein (1991), Longford (1993), and Hedeker & Gibbons (1994).

The approach can be presented heuristically by computing a "linearized dependent variable" as in the generalized linear model of McCullagh & Nelder (1989). Basically, the analysis involves use of a standard HLM model with the introduction of a special weighting at level-1. However, after this standard HLM analysis has converged, the linearized dependent variable and the weights must be recomputed. Then, the standard HLM analysis is re-computed. This iterative process of HLM analyses and re-computing weights and linearized dependent variable continues until estimates converge.

We term the standard HLM iterations "micro-iterations." The recomputation of the linearized dependent variable and the weights constitute a "macro iteration." The approach is outlined below for four cases: Bernoulli (binomial with $n_{ij} = 1$), Poisson with $n_{ij} = 1$, binomial with $n_{ij} > 1$, and Poisson with $n_{ij} > 1$.

Bernoulli (binomial with $n_{ij} = 1$). Consider the model

$$Y_{ij} = \mu_{ij} + \epsilon_{ij} \tag{5.12}$$

with μ_{ij} defined as in Equation 5.8 and

$$E(\epsilon_{ij}) = 0 \qquad Var(\epsilon_{ij}) = w_{ij} = \mu_{ij}(1 - \mu_{ij}) . \tag{5.13}$$

We now substitute for μ_{ij} its linear approximation

$$\mu_{ij} \approx \mu_{ij}^{(0)} + \frac{\partial \mu_{ij}}{\partial \eta_{ij}}(\eta_{ij} - \eta_{ij}^{(0)}) \tag{5.14}$$

with

$$\eta_{ij}^{(0)} = \log\Big(\frac{\eta_{ij}^{(0)}}{1 - \mu_{ij}^{(0)}}\Big) , \tag{5.15}$$

where $\mu_{ij}^{(0)}$ is an initial estimate and

$$\frac{\partial \mu_{ij}}{\partial \eta_{ij}} = w_{ij} = \mu_{ij}(1 - \mu_{ij}) . \tag{5.16}$$

If we evaluate w_{ij} at its initial estimates

$$w_{ij}^{(0)} = \mu_{ij}^{(0)}(1 - \mu_{ij}^{(0)}),$$ (5.17)

(5.12) can be written as

$$Y_{ij} = \mu_{ij}^{(0)} + w_{ij}^{(0)}(\eta_{ij} - \eta_{ij}^{(0)}) + \epsilon_{ij}.$$ (5.18)

Algebraically rearranging the equation so that all observables are on the left-hand side yields

$$Z_{ij}^{(0)} = \eta_{ij} + \frac{\epsilon_{ij}}{w_{ij}^{(0)}}$$ (5.19)

$$= \beta_{0j} + \beta_{1j}X_{1ij} + \beta_{2ij}X_{2ij} + \cdots + \beta_{Qij}X_{Qij} + e_{ij}$$

where

$$Z_{ij}^{(0)} = \frac{Y_{ij} - \mu_{ij}^{(0)}}{w_{ij}^{(0)}} + \eta_{ij}^{(0)}$$ (5.20)

is the linearized dependent variable and

$$Var(e_{ij}) = Var\left(\frac{\epsilon_{ij}}{w_{ij}^{(0)}}\right) \approx \frac{1}{w_{ij}^{(0)}}.$$ (5.21)

Thus, (5.19) is a standard HLM level-1 model with outcome $Z_{ij}^{(0)}$ and level-1 weighting variable $w_{ij}^{(0)}$.

The algorithm works as follows.

1. Given initial estimates of the predicted value, μ_{ij}, and therefore of the linearized dependent variable, Z_{ij}, and the weight, w_{ij}, compute a weighted HLM analysis with (5.19) as the level-1 model.
2. The HLM analysis from step 1 will produce new predicted values and thus new linearized dependent variables and weights. HLM will now compute a new, re-weighted SSM file with the appropriate linearized dependent variable and weights.

3. Based on the new linearized dependent variable and weights, re-compute step 1.

This process goes on until the linearized dependent variable, the weights, and therefore, the parameter estimates, converge to a prespecified tolerance. The program then stops.

Poisson with $n_{ij} = 1$. The procedure is exactly the same as in the binomial case with $n_{ij} = 1$ except that

$$\text{Var}(\epsilon_{ij}) = w_{ij} \; \frac{\partial \mu_{ij}}{\partial \eta_{ij}} = \mu_{ij} \; . \tag{5.22}$$

Binomial with $n_{ij} > 1$. In the previous example, Y_{ij} was formally the number of successes in one trial and therefore could take on a value of 0 or 1. We now consider the case where Y_{ij} is the number of successes in n_{ij} trials, where Y_{ij} and n_{ij} are non-negative integers, $Y_{ij} \leq n_{ij}$.

Suppose that a researcher is interested in examining the relationship between pre-school experience (yes or no) and grade retention and wonders whether this relationship is similar for males and females. The design involves students at level 1 nested within schools at level 2. In this case, each school would have four "cell counts" (boys with and without pre-school and girls with and without pre-school). Thus, the data could be organized so that every school had four observations (except possibly schools without variation on pre-school or sex), where each observation was a cell having a cell size n_{ij} and a cell count Y_{ij} of students in that cell who were, in fact, retained. One could then re-conceptualize the study as having up to four level-1 units (cells); the outcome Y_{ij}, given the cell probability ϕ_{ij} would be distributed as $\text{B}(n_{ij}, \phi_{ij})$. There would be three level-1 predictors (a contrast for pre-school experience, a contrast for sex, and an interaction contrast). This problem then has the structure of a $2 \times 2 \times J$ contingency table (pre-school experience by sex by school) with the last factor viewed as random.

The structure of a level-1 file for group 2 might appear as follows.

Group	ID	n_{ij}	Y_{ij}	X_{1ij}	X_{2ij}	X_{3ij}
Girls with pre-school	2	n_{12}	Y_{12}	.5	.5	.25
Girls without pre-school	2	n_{22}	Y_{22}	.5	$-.5$	$-.25$
Boys with pre-school	2	n_{32}	Y_{32}	$-.5$	.5	$-.25$
Boys without pre-school	2	n_{42}	Y_{42}	$-.5$	$-.5$	.25

For example, n_{12} is the number of girls in school 2 with pre-school and Y_{12} is the number of those girls who were retained. The predictor X_{1ij} is a contrast coefficient to assess the effect of sex (.5 if female, $-.5$ if male); X_{2ij} is a contrast for pre-school experience (.5 if yes, $-.5$ if no), and $X_{3ij} = X_{1ij} * X_{2ij}$ is the interaction contrast.

Estimation works the same in this case as in the binomial case except that

$$Z_{ij} = \frac{Y_{ij} - n_{ij}\mu_{ij}}{w_{ij}} + \eta_{ij} \qquad (5.23)$$

with

$$w_{ij} = n_{ij}\mu_{ij}(1 - \mu_{ij}) . \qquad (5.24)$$

Poisson with $n_{ij} > 1$. Consider now a study of the number of homicides committed within each of j neighborhoods in a large city. Many neighborhoods will have no homocides. The expected number of homocides in a neighborhood will depend not only on the homicide rate for that neighborhood, but also on the size of that neighborhood as indexed, perhaps, by its number of residents, n_{ij}. Level-1 variables might include characteristics of the homicide (e.g., whether the homicide involved a domestic dispute, whether it involved use of a gun). Each cell (e.g., the four types of homicide as defined by the cross-classification of domestic (yes or no) and use of a gun (yes or no) would be a level-1 unit.

Estimation in this case is the same as in the Poisson case with $n_{ij} = 1$ except that

$$Z_{ij} = \frac{Y_{ij} - n_{ij}\mu_{ij}}{w_{ij}} + \eta_{ij} \qquad (5.25)$$

and

$$w_{ij} = n_{ij}\mu_{ij} . \qquad (5.26)$$

Properties of the estimators. HGLM produces approximate empirical Bayes estimates of the randomly-varying level-1 coefficients, generalized least squares estimators of the level-2 (and level-3) coefficients, and approximate restricted maximum-likelihood estimators of the variance and covariance parameters. Yang (1995) has conducted a simulation study of these estimators in comparison with an alternative approach used by some programs that sets the level-2 random coefficients to zero in computing the linearized dependent variables. Breslow & Clayton (1993) refer to this alternative approach as "marginalized quasi-likelihood" or MQL. Rodriquez & Goldman (1995) had found that MQL produced biased estimates of the level-2 variance and the level-2 regression coefficients. Yang's results showed a substantial improvement (reduction in bias and mean squared error) in using the approach of HGLM. In particular, the bias in estimation of the level-2 coefficients was never more than 10 percent for HGLM, while the MQL approach commonly produced a bias between 10 and 20 percent. HGLM performed better than the alternative approach in estimating a level-2 variance component as well. However, a negative bias was found in estimating this variance component, ranging between two percent and 21 percent. The bias was most severe when the true variance was very large and the typical "probability of success" was very small (or, equivalently, very large). Initial simulation results under the Poisson model appear somewhat more favorable than these. Breslow & Clayton (1993) suggest that the estimation will be more efficient as n_{ij} increases.

Unit-specific and population-average models

The models described above have been termed "unit-specific" models. They model the expected outcome for a level-2 unit conditional on a given set of random effects. For example, in the Bernoulli case ($n_{ij} = 1$), we might have a level-1 (within-school) model

$$\eta_{ij} = \beta_{0j} + \beta_{1j}X_{ij} , \qquad (5.27)$$

and a level-2 (between-school) model

$$\beta_{0j} = \gamma_{00} + \gamma_{01}W_{ij} + u_{0j} \qquad (5.28)$$
$$\beta_{1j} = \gamma_{10}$$

leading to the combined model

$$\eta_{ij} = \gamma_{00} + \gamma_{01} W_{ij} + \gamma_{10} X_{ij} + u_{0j} \,. \qquad (5.29)$$

Under this model, the predicted probability for case ij, given u_{0j} would be

$$E(Y_{ij}|u_{0j}) = \frac{1}{1 + \exp\{-(\gamma_{00} + \gamma_{01} W_{ij} + \gamma_{10} X_{ij} + u_0 j)\}} \,. \qquad (5.30)$$

In this model γ_{10} is the expected difference in the log-odds of "success" between two students who attend the same school but differ by one unit on X; γ_{01} is the expected difference in the log-odds of success between two students who have the same value on X but attend schools differing by one unit on W (holding $u_0 j$ constant). These definitions parallel definitions used in a standard HLM for continuous outcomes.

However, one might also want to know the average difference between log-odds of success of students having the same X but attending schools differing by one unit on W, that is, the difference of interest *averaging over all possible values of $u_0 j$*. In this case, the unit-specific model would not be appropriate. The model that would be appropriate would be a "population-average" model (Zeger, Liang, & Albert, 1988). The distinction is tricky in part because it does not arise in the standard HLM (with an identity link function). It arises only in the case of a nonlinear link function.

Using the same example as above, the population average model would be

$$E(Y_{ij}) = \frac{1}{1 + \exp\{-(\gamma_{00}^* + \gamma_{01}^* W_{ij} + \gamma_{10}^* X_{ij})\}} \,. \qquad (5.31)$$

Notice that (5.31) does not condition on (or "hold constant") the random effect u_{0j}. Thus, γ_{01}^* gives the expected difference in log-odds of success between two students with the same X who attend schools differing by one unit on W — without respect to the random effect, u_{0j}. If one had a nationally representative sample and could validly assign a causal inference to W, γ_{01}^* would be the change in the log-odds of success in the whole society associated with boosting W by one unit while γ_{01} would be the change in log-odds associated with boosting W one unit for those schools sharing the same value of u_{0j}.

HGLM produces estimates for both the unit-specific and population-average models. The population-average results are based on generalized least squares given the variance-covariance estimates from the unit-specific model. Moreover, HGLM produces robust standard error estimates for the population-average model (Zeger, *et al.*, 1988). These standard errors are relatively insensitive to misspecification of the variances and covariances at the two levels and to the distributional assumptions at each level. The method of estimation used in HGLM for the population-average model is equivalent to the "generalized estimating equation" (GEE) approach popularized by Zeger, *et al.* (1988).

The following differences between unit-specific and population-average results are to be expected:

- ❑ If all predictors are held constant at their means, and if their means are zero, the population-average intercept can be used to estimate the average probability of success across the entire population, that is

$$\hat{\mu}_{ij} = \frac{1}{1 + \exp\{-\gamma_{00}^*\}} \, . \tag{5.32}$$

This will not be true of unit-specific intercepts unless the average probability of success is very close to .5.

- ❑ Coefficient estimates (other than the intercept) based on the population-average model will often tend to be similar to those based on the unit-specific model but will tend to be smaller in absolute value.

Users will need to take care in choosing unit-specific versus population-average results for their research. Choice will depend on the specific research questions that are of interest. In the previous example, if one was primarily interested in how a change in W can be expected to affect a particular individual school's mean, one would use the unit-specific model. If one were interested in how a change in W can be expected to affect the overall population mean, one would use the population-average model.

Extra-binomial or extra-Poisson dispersion at level 1. As mentioned earlier, if the data follow the assumed level-1 sampling model, the level-1 variance of the Y_{ij} will be w_{ij} where

$$w_{ij} = n_{ij}\mu_{ij}(1 - \mu_{ij}), \qquad \textit{Binomial case, or}$$

$$w_{ij} = n_{ij}\mu_{ij}, \qquad \textit{Poisson case .}$$

However, if the level-1 data do not follow this model, the actual level-1 variance may be larger than that assumed (over-dispersion) or smaller than that assumed (under-dispersion). For example, if undetected clustering exists within level-1 units or if the level-1 model is under-specified, extra-binomial or extra-Poisson dispersion may arise. This problem can be handled in a variety of ways; HGLM allows estimation of a scalar variance so that the level-1 variance will be $\sigma^2 w_{ij}$.[1]

Restricted versus full PQL. The default method of estimation for the two-level HGLM is restricted PQL, while full PQL is an option. For the three-level HGLM, estimation is by means of full PQL only.

Hypothesis testing

The logic of hypothesis testing with HGLM is quite similar to that used in the case of HLM. Thus, for the fixed effects (the γ's), a table of approximate t-values is routinely printed for univariate tests; multivariate tests for the fixed effects are available using the approach described earlier in Chapter 2 above. Similarly, univariate test for variance components (approximate chi-squares) are also routinely printed out. The one exception is that multivariate tests based on comparing model deviances ($-2*\textit{log-likelihood at convergence}$) are not available using HGLM, because HGLM is based on quasi-likelihood rather than maximum-likelihood estimation.

---

[1]Extra-binomial dispersion is allowed only for $n > 1$ while extra-Poisson variation is allowed for $n = 1$ and for $n > 1$. This distinction is in conformity to the properties of a beta-binomial distribution, which admits over-dispersion only for $n > 1$; and for the Poisson-gamma model, which admits over-dispersion for $n = 1$ and for $n > 1$.

HGLM: CONCEPTUAL AND STATISTICAL BACKGROUND

6   Fitting HGLMs (Nonlinear Models)

There is no difference between HGLM ("nonlinear analysis") and HLM ("linear analysis") in the construction of the SSM file. Thus, the same SSM file can be used for nonlinear and linear analysis.

Executing nonlinear analyses based on the SSM file

Model specification for nonlinear analyses, as in the case of linear analyses, can be achieved through interactive execution, batch execution, or via Windows (PC implementation only). The mechanics of model specification are generally the same as in linear analyses with the following differences:

1. In the case of nonlinear analysis, the level-1 data file must remain in the directory in which it was located when the SSM file was made, and it must keep the same filename. This is because nonlinear analysis, unlike linear analysis, requires access to the raw level-1 data (these data are read anew at each macro iteration).

2. The user has an option of four types of nonlinear analysis (two for dichotomous outcomes and two for count outcomes).

3. The user may wish to allow extra-binomial or extra-Poisson dispersion.

4. As mentioned, the nonlinear analysis is doubly iterative so the maximum number of macro iterations must be specified as well as the maximum number of micro iterations.

Similarly, convergence criteria can be reset for macro iterations as well as micro iterations.[1]

Below we provide two detailed examples of nonlinear analyses: the first uses the Bernoulli model, that is, a binomial model with the number of trials, n_{ij}, equal to one. The second example uses a binomial model with $n_{ij} > 1$. The analogs of these two analyses for count data are, respectively, the Poisson model with equal exposure and the Poisson case with variable exposure (some brief notes about these two applications are also included). Interactive and batch specification are illustrated.

Case 1: a Bernoulli model

Data are from a national survey of primary education in Thailand (see Raudenbush & Bhumirat, 1992, for details), conducted in 1988, and yielding, for our analysis, complete data on 7516 sixth graders nested within 356 primary schools. Of interest is the probability that a child will repeat a grade during the primary years ($REP1 = 1$ if yes, 0 if no). It is hypothesized that the sex of the child ($SEX = 1$ if male, 0 of female), the child's pre-primary experience ($PPED = 1$ if yes, 0 if no), and the school mean SES ($MSESC$) will be associated with the probability of repetition. Every level-1 record corresponds to a student, with a single binary outcome per student, so the model type is Bernoulli.

These data are provided along with the HLM software so that users may replicate our results in order to assure that the program is operating correctly.

Below is the interactive session for the analysis. As usual, annotations are in *italics*, and user responses are typed in a swiss font.

---

[1]The overall accuracy of the parameter estimates is determined by the convergence criterion for macro iterations. The convergence criterion for micro iterations will influence the number of micro iterations per macro iteration. The default specifications stop macro iterations when the largest parameter estimate change is less than 10^{-4}; micro iterations within macro iterations stop when the conditional log likelihood (conditional on the current weights and values of the linearized dependent variable) changes by less than 10^{-5}.

```
Do you want to do a nonlinear analysis?  Y
Enter type of nonlinear analysis:

     1) Bernoulli (0 or 1)
     2) Binomial (count)
     3) Poisson  (constant exposure)
     4) Poisson  (variable exposure)

type of analysis:  1

Enter number of macro iterations 25
Enter number of micro iterations 20
```

*As mentioned, with one binary outcome per level-1 unit, the model choice is
"1" (Bernoulli). In the next section, we have an example where every level-
1 record has a number of "successes" in n_{ij} "trials," in which case the
choice will be "2" (binomial). Specifying 25 macro iterations sets an upper
limit; if, after the 25th iteration the algorithm has not converged. The
program will nonetheless terminate and print the results at that iteration.
Similarly, setting 20 as the number of micro iterations insures that, after
20 micro iterations, the current macro iteration will terminate even if the
micro iteration convergence criterion has not been met.*

```
                    SPECIFYING A LEVEL-1 OUTCOME VARIABLE

Please specify a level-1 outcome variable
 The choices are:
 For      SEX enter  1    For     PPED enter  2    For     REP1 enter  3

What is the outcome variable:  3

Do you wish to:

    Examine means,variances,chi-squared, etc? Enter 1
    Specify an HLM model?                      Enter 2
    Define a new outcome variable?             Enter 3
    Exit?                                      Enter 4
What do you want to do?  2


                    SPECIFYING AN HLM MODEL

Level-1 predictor variable specification

Which level-1 predictors do you wish to use?
```

```
The choices are:
For     SEX enter  1     For      PPED enter  2

level-1 predictor? (Enter 0 to end)   1
level-1 predictor? (Enter 0 to end)   2
level-1 predictor? (Enter 0 to end)   0
```

Thus, we have set up a level-1 model with repetition (REP1) as the outcome and with sex (SEX) and pre-primary experience (PPED) as predictors.

```
Do you want to center any level-1 predictors?  n

Do you want to set the level-1 intercept to zero in this analysis?  n


Level-2 predictor variable specification

Which level-2 variables do you wish to use?
 The choices are:
 For    MSESC enter  1

 Which level-2 predictors to model INTRCPT1?
  Level-2 predictor? (Enter 0 to end)    1
 Which level-2 predictors to model     SEX slope?
  Level-2 predictor? (Enter 0 to end)   0
 Which level-2 predictors to model    PPED slope?
  Level-2 predictor? (Enter 0 to end)   0

Do you want to constrain the variances in any of the level-2 random
 effects to zero?  y
 Do you want to fix INTRCPT1?  n
 Do you want to fix       SEX?  y
 Do you want to fix      PPED?  y

 Do you want to center any level-2 predictors?  y
 (Enter 0 for no centering, 2 for grand-mean)

 How do you want to center    MSESC?  2
```

Thus we have modeled the level-1 intercept as depending on the mean SES (MSESC) of the school. The coefficients associated with sex and pre-primary experience are fixed. Mean SES has been centered around its grand mean.

```
                    ADDITIONAL PROGRAM FEATURES

Select the level-2 variables that you might consider for
inclusion as predictors in subsequent models.
```

```
The choices are:
For    MSESC enter  1

Which level-2 variables to model INTRCPT1?
 Level-2 variable? (Enter 0 to end)  0

                        OUTPUT SPECIFICATION

 Enter a problem title:  Bernoulli output, Thailand data
 Enter name of output file:  thaibern.lis
```

Thus concludes the interactive terminal session. Below we provide a transcript of the messages that come to the screen during computation of the results.

```
                      MACRO ITERATION 1

Computing . . ., please wait
Starting values computed.  Iterations begun.
Should you wish to terminate the iterations prior to convergence, enter cntl-c
The value of the likelihood function at iteration 1 = -2.417683E+003
The value of the likelihood function at iteration 2 = -2.417538E+003
The value of the likelihood function at iteration 3 = -2.417509E+003
The value of the likelihood function at iteration 4 = -2.417502E+003
The value of the likelihood function at iteration 5 = -2.417501E+003
The value of the likelihood function at iteration 6 = -2.417501E+003
```

Macro iteration number 1 has converged after six micro iterations. This macro iteration actually computes the linear-model estimates (using the identity link function as if the level-1 errors were assumed normal). These results are then transformed and input to start macro iteration 2, which is, in fact, the first nonlinear iteration.

```
                      MACRO ITERATION 2

Computing . . ., please wait
Starting values computed.  Iterations begun.
Should you wish to terminate the iterations prior to convergence, enter cntl-c
The value of the likelihood function at iteration 1 = -1.011299E+004
The value of the likelihood function at iteration 2 = -1.011291E+004
The value of the likelihood function at iteration 3 = -1.011288E+004
The value of the likelihood function at iteration 4 = -1.011287E+004
The value of the likelihood function at iteration 5 = -1.011287E+004
The value of the likelihood function at iteration 6 = -1.011287E+004
```

Macro interation 2, the first nonlinear macro iteration, also converged after six micro iterations.

```
Computing . . ., please wait
Starting values computed.  Iterations begun.
Should you wish to terminate the iterations prior to convergence, enter cntl-c
The value of the likelihood function at iteration 1 = -1.001398E+004
The value of the likelihood function at iteration 2 = -1.001398E+004
```

Note that macro iteration 9 converged with just 2 micro iterations. Also, the change in parameter estimates between macro iterations 8 and 9 was found negligible (less than the criterion for convergence) so that macro iteration 9 was the final "unit-specific" macro iteration. One final "population-average" iteration is computed, and screen output for that is given below.

MACRO ITERATION 10

```
Computing . . ., please wait
Starting values computed.  Iterations begun.
Should you wish to terminate the iterations prior to convergence, enter cntl-c
The value of the likelihood function at iteration 1 = -1.011354E+004
The value of the likelihood function at iteration 2 = -1.011354E+004
```

This completes the terminal output for the analysis. Next, we examine the output file `thaibern.lis`.

```
****************************************************************
*                                                            *
*         H  H  L      M    M    22                          *
*         H  H  L      MM  MM   2  2                         *
*         HHHHH  L      M  M  M     2      Version 4.01       *
*         H  H  L      M    M     2                          *
*         H  H  LLLLL  M    M  2222                          *
*                                                            *
****************************************************************
```

SPECIFICATIONS FOR THIS NONLINEAR HLM RUN   Thu Feb 8 18:19:11 1996

```
Problem Title: bernoulli output, Thailand data

The data source for this run = thaiugrp.ssm
Output file name            = thaibern.lis
The maximum number of level-2 units = 356
The maximum number of micro iterations = 20
Method of estimation: restricted PQL
Maximum number of macro iterations = 25
```

```
Distribution at Level-1: Bernoulli

The outcome variable is REP1

The model specified for the fixed effects was:
_____

     Level-1                  Level-2
     Coefficients             Predictors
     _____              _____

         INTRCPT1, B0         INTRCPT2, G00
$                                MSESC, G01
#        SEX slope, B1        INTRCPT2, G10
#        PPED slope, B2       INTRCPT2, G20

'#' - The residual parameter variance for this level-1 coefficient has been set
      to zero.
'$' - This level-2 predictor has been centered around its grand mean.

The model specified for the covariance components was:
_____

         Tau dimensions
           INTRCPT1


Summary of the model specified (in equation format)
_____

Level-1 Model

    Prob(Y=1|B) = P
```

*This is the program's way of saying that the level-1 sampling model is
Bernoulli; the above equation, written with subscripts and Greek letters, is*

$$\text{Prob}(Y_{ij} = 1|\boldsymbol{\beta}_j) = \phi_{ij} \ .$$

```
    log[P/(1-P)] = B0 + B1*(SEX) + B2*(PPED)
```

Thus, the level-1 structural model is

$$\eta_{ij} = \log\left[\frac{\phi_{ij}}{1 - \phi_{ij}}\right] = \beta_{0j} + \beta_{1j}(SEX)_{ij} + \beta_{2j}(PPED)_{ij} \ .$$

Level-2 Model

```
B0 = G00 + G01*(MSESC) + U0
B1 = G10
B2 = G20
```

The level-2 structural model is

$$\begin{aligned}
\beta_{0j} &= \gamma_{00} + \gamma_{01}(MSESC)_j + u_{0j} \\
\beta_{1j} &= \gamma_{10} \\
\beta_{2j} &= \gamma_{20} \, .
\end{aligned}$$

```
Level-1 variance = 1/[P(1-P)]
```

In the metric of the linearized dependent variable, the level-1 variance is the reciprocal of the Bernoulli variance, $\phi_{ij}(1 - \phi_{ij})$.

Three sets of output results appear below: those for the normal linear model with identity link function, those for the unit-specific model with logit link function, and those for the population-average model with logit link. Typically, only the latter 2 sets of results will be relevant for drawing conclusions. The linear model with identity link is estimated simply to obtain starting values for the estimation of the models with logit-link.

RESULTS FOR LINEAR MODEL WITH THE IDENTITY LINK FUNCTION

Sigma—squared =   0.12181

Tau
 INTRCPT1   0.01897

Tau (as correlations)
 INTRCPT1 1.000

Random level-1 coefficient   Reliability estimate

 INTRCPT1, B0   0.749

The value of the likelihood function at iteration 6 = -2.417501E+003

The outcome variable is   REP1

Estimation of fixed effects: (linear model with identity link function)

Fixed Effect	Coefficient	Standard Error	T-ratio	P-value
For INTRCPT1, B0				
INTRCPT2, G00	0.153756	0.010812	14.221	0.000
MSESC, G01	-0.033414	0.022465	-1.487	0.137
For SEX slope, B1				
INTRCPT2, G10	0.054131	0.008330	6.498	0.000
For PPED slope, B2				
INTRCPT2, G20	-0.064613	0.010926	-5.914	0.000

RESULTS FOR NONLINEAR MODEL WITH THE LOGIT LINK FUNCTION: Unit-Specific Model
(macro iteration 9)

Tau
INTRCPT1   1.29570

Tau (as correlations)
INTRCPT1 1.000

Random level-1 coefficient	Reliability estimate
INTRCPT1, B0	0.682

The value of the likelihood function at iteration 2 = -1.001398E+004

The outcome variable is   REP1

Final estimation of fixed effects: (Unit-specific model)

Fixed Effect	Coefficient	Standard Error	T-ratio	P-value
For INTRCPT1, B0				
INTRCPT2, G00	-2.046960	0.093984	-21.780	0.000
MSESC, G01	-0.254412	0.193318	-1.316	0.188
For SEX slope, B1				
INTRCPT2, G10	0.508561	0.073935	6.879	0.000
For PPED slope, B2				
INTRCPT2, G20	-0.594375	0.095962	-6.194	0.000

Final estimation of variance components:

Random Effect	Standard Deviation	Variance Component	df	Chi-square	P-value
INTRCPT1, U0	1.13829	1.29570	354	1431.43038	0.000

```
RESULTS FOR NONLINEAR MODEL WITH THE LOGIT LINK FUNCTION:
Population Average Model

Tau
  INTRCPT1      1.29570

Tau (as correlations)
  INTRCPT1  1.000
```

Random level-1 coefficient	Reliability estimate
INTRCPT1, B0	0.760

```
The value of the likelihood function at iteration 2 = -1.011354E+004


The outcome variable is      REP1

Final estimation of fixed effects: (Population-average model)
```

Fixed Effect	Coefficient	Standard Error	T-ratio	P-value
For INTRCPT1, B0				
INTRCPT2, G00	-1.748402	0.087969	-19.875	0.000
MSESC, G01	-0.283620	0.185179	-1.532	0.125
For SEX slope, B1				
INTRCPT2, G10	0.446546	0.066993	6.666	0.000
For PPED slope, B2				
INTRCPT2, G20	-0.536379	0.088479	-6.062	0.000

Notice that the results for the population-average model are quite similar to the results for the unit-specific model except in the case of the intercept. The intercept in the population-average model in this case is the expected log-odds of repetition for a person with values of zero on the predictors (and therefore, for a female without pre-primary experience attending a school of average SES). In this case, this expected log-odds corresponds to a probability of $1/(1 + \exp\{1.748402\}) = .148$, which is "population-average" repetition rate for this group. In contrast, the unit-specific intercept is the expected log-odds of repetition rate for the same kind of student, but one who attends a school that not only has a mean SES of 0, but also has a random effect of zero — that is, a school with a "typical" repetition rate for the school of its type. This conditional expected log-odds is -2.046960, corresponding to a probability of $1/(1 + \exp\{2.046960\}) = .114$. Thus the probability of repetition is lower in a school with a random effect of zero than the average in the population of schools having mean SES of zero *taken as a whole. This is a typical result. Population-average probabilities will be closer to .50 (than will the corresponding unit-specific probabilities).*

One final set of results is printed out: population-average results with robust standard errors (below). Note that the robust standard errors in this case are very similar to the model-based standard errors, with a slight increase for the level-2 predictor and slight decreases for level-1 predictors. Results for other data may not follow this pattern.

```
The outcome variable is     REP1

Final estimation of fixed effects
(Population-average model with robust standard errors)
```

Fixed Effect	Coefficient	Standard Error	T-ratio	P-value
For INTRCPT1, B0				
INTRCPT2, G00	-1.748402	0.082158	-21.281	0.000
MSESC, G01	-0.283620	0.196005	-1.447	0.148
For SEX slope, B1				
INTRCPT2, G10	0.446546	0.062788	7.112	0.000
For PPED slope, B2				
INTRCPT2, G20	-0.536379	0.082221	-6.524	0.000

Batch execution

The interactive session annotated above produced the following command file (newcmd.hlm).

```
#This command file was run with thaiugrp.ssm
LEVEL1:REP1=INTRCPT1+SEX+PPED+RANDOM
LEVEL2:INTRCPT1=INTRCPT2+MSESC,2+RANDOM/
LEVEL2:SEX=INTRCPT2/
LEVEL2:PPED=INTRCPT2/
RESFIL:N
STOPMICRO:0.000010
STOPMACRO:0.000100
MACROIT:25
MICROIT:20
NONLIN:BERNOULLI
LEV1OLS:0
HYPOTH:n
FIXTAU:3
CONSTRAIN:N
OUTPUT:thaibern.lis
TITLE:Bernoulli output, Thailand data
ACCEL:5
```

If one types at the DOS prompt:

```
hlm21 thaiugrp.ssm newcmd.hlm
```

the output above would be reproduced. It is a good idea to rename the newcmd.hlm file if it is to be edited and re-used. Each execution of the program will produce a newcmd.hlm file that will overwrite the old one.

Note that the newcmd.hlm file above is similar to the same file produced by a linear-model analysis, with the addition of the following lines:

```
STOPMICRO:0.000010        default convergence criterion for micro iterations
STOPMACRO:0.000100        default convergence criterion for micro iterations
MACROIT:25                   maximum number if macro iterations
MICROIT:20      maximum number if micro iterations per macro iteration
NONLIN:BERNOULLI                         type of nonlinear model
```

Case 2: a binomial model (number of trials, $n_{ij} > 1$)

A familiar example of a two-level binomial data is the number of hits, Y_{ij}, in game i for baseball player j based on n_{ij} at bats. In an experimental setting, a subject j under condition i might produce Y_{ij} successes in n_{ij} trials.

A common use of a binomial model is when analysts do not have access to the raw data at level 1. For example, one might know the proportion of children passing a criterion-referenced test within each of many schools. This proportion might be broken down within schools by sex and grade. A binomial model could be used to analyze such data. The cases would be sex-by-age "cells" within each school where Y_{ij} is the number passing within cell i of school j and n_{ij} is the number of "trials," that is, the number of children in that cell. Sex and grade would be level-1 predictors.

Indeed, in the previous example, although raw level-1 data were available, the two level-1 predictors, sex and pre-primary experience, were categorical. For illustration, we reorganized these data so that each school had, potentially, four cells defined by the cross-classification of sex and pre-primary experience:

☐ females without pre-primary experience,

☐ females with pre-primary experience,

☐ males without pre-primary experience, and

☐ males with pre-primary experience.

Level-1 predictors were the same as before, with $SEX = 1$ if male, 0 if female; $PPED = 1$ if pre-primary experience, 0 if not. The outcome is the number of children retained in a particular cell, and we created a variable $TRIAL$, which is the number of children in each cell. In some schools there were no children of a certain type (*e.g.*, no females with pre-primary experience). Such schools would have fewer than four cells. The interactive session for executing the analysis is given below.

```
Do you want to do a nonlinear analysis?  Y

Enter type of nonlinear analysis:

    1) Bernoulli (0 or 1)
    2) Binomial (count)
    3) Poisson  (constant exposure)
    4) Poisson  (variable exposure)

type of analysis:  2

Enter number of macro iterations  25
Enter number of micro iterations  20

Do you wish to allow overdispersion at level 1?  N
```

For binomial models with $n_{ij} > 1$ and for all Poisson models, a level-1 dispersion parameter, σ^2, may optionally be estimated. If the assumed model holds, $\sigma^2 = 1.0$. If the data are overdispersed, $\sigma^2 > 1.0$; if the data are underdispersed, $\sigma^2 < 1.0$.

```
                SPECIFYING A LEVEL-1 OUTCOME VARIABLE

Please specify a level-1 outcome variable

 The choices are:
 For      SEX enter  1     For      PPED enter  2     For      REP1 enter  3
 For    TRIAL enter  4

What is the outcome variable:  3
```

```
Do you wish to:

    Examine means,variances,chi-squared, etc? Enter 1
    Specify an HLM model?                      Enter 2
    Define a new outcome variable?             Enter 3
    Exit?                                      Enter 4

What do you want to do?  2


                        SPECIFYING AN HLM MODEL

Level-1 predictor variable specification

Which level-1 predictors do you wish to use?

 The choices are:
 For     SEX enter  1    For     PPED enter  2
 For   TRIAL enter  4

 level-1 predictor? (Enter 0 to end)   1
 level-1 predictor? (Enter 0 to end)   2
 level-1 predictor? (Enter 0 to end)   0

For the nonlinear analysis, which variable indicates the number of trials?  4
```

*As mentioned, in this case "trial" is a variable created to indicate how
many children were in a given cell. The above question does not appear
in a Bernoulli analysis for which the number of trials is, by definition, 1.
Other aspects of the terminal session are identical to what we saw in Case 1
and so will not be reproduced here.*

The output follows.

```
        ****************************************************************
        *                                                              *
        *       H   H  L      M   M   22                               *
        *       H   H  L      MM MM  2  2                              *
        *       HHHHH  L      M M M    2        Version 4.01           *
        *       H   H  L      M   M    2                               *
        *       H   H  LLLLL  M   M   2222                             *
        *                                                              *
        ****************************************************************

SPECIFICATIONS FOR THIS NONLINEAR HLM RUN          Thu Feb  8 18:30:02 1996
```
_____

```
Problem Title: BINOMIAL ANALYSIS, THAILAND DATA
```

```
The data source for this run = thaigrp.ssm
Output file name             = thaibnml.lis
The maximum number of level-2 units = 356
The maximum number of micro iterations = 50
Method of estimation: restricted PQL
Maximum number of macro iterations = 50


Distribution at Level-1: Binomial

The outcome variable is REP1

The model specified for the fixed effects was:
```

```
Level-1                      Level-2
Coefficients                 Predictors
```

	Level-1 Coefficients	Level-2 Predictors
	INTRCPT1, B0	INTRCPT2, G00
$		MSESC, G01
#	SEX slope, B1	INTRCPT2, G10
#	PPED slope, B2	INTRCPT2, G20

'#' - The residual parameter variance for this level-1 coefficient has been set
      to zero.
'$' - This level-2 predictor has been centered around its grand mean.

The model specified for the covariance components was:

```
        Tau dimensions
            INTRCPT1
```

Summary of the model specified (in equation format)

Level-1 Model

```
    E(Y|B) = TRIAL*P
    V(Y|B) = TRIAL*P(1-P)
```

This is the program's way of saying that the level-1 sampling model is binomial with "TRIAL" indicating the number of trials, so that the above equation, written with subscripts and Greek letters, is

$$E(Y_{ij}|\boldsymbol{\beta}_j) = n_{ij}\phi_{ij}$$
$$\mathsf{Var}(Y_{ij}|\boldsymbol{\beta}_j) = n_{ij}\phi_{ij}(1 - \phi_{ij}),$$

where $n_{ij} = TRIAL$.

```
        log[P/(1-P)] = B0 + B1*(SEX) + B2*(PPED)

Level-2 Model

    B0 = G00 + G01*(MSESC) + U0
    B1 = G10
    B2 = G20
```

Notice that the level-1 and level-2 structural models are identical to those in Case 1.

```
Level-1 variance = 1/[TRIAL*P(1-P)]
```

In the metric of the linearized dependent variable, the level-1 variance is the reciprocal of the binomial variance,

$$n_{ij}\phi_{ij}(1 - \phi_{ij}) \,.$$

Results for the unit-specific model, population-average model, and population-average model with robust standard errors, are given below. A comparison with the results for Case 1 will show that the results are essentially identical.

```
RESULTS FOR NONLINEAR MODEL WITH THE LOGIT LINK FUNCTION: Unit-Specific Model
(macro iteration 9)

The outcome variable is      REP1
```

Final estimation of fixed effects: (Unit-specific model)

Fixed Effect	Coefficient	Standard Error	T-ratio	P-value
For INTRCPT1, B0				
INTRCPT2, G00	-2.046963	0.093985	-21.780	0.000
MSESC, G01	-0.254413	0.193319	-1.316	0.188
For SEX slope, B1				
INTRCPT2, G10	0.508562	0.073935	6.879	0.000
For PPED slope, B2				
INTRCPT2, G20	-0.594375	0.095962	-6.194	0.000

Final estimation of variance components:

Random Effect		Standard Deviation	Variance Component	df	Chi-square	P-value
INTRCPT1,	U0	1.13829	1.29571	354	1431.43155	0.000

```
RESULTS FOR NONLINEAR MODEL WITH THE LOGIT LINK FUNCTION:
Population Average Model

The outcome variable is      REP1

Final estimation of fixed effects: (Population-average model)
```

Fixed Effect	Coefficient	Standard Error	T-ratio	P-value
For INTRCPT1, B0				
INTRCPT2, G00	-1.748402	0.087969	-19.875	0.000
MSESC, G01	-0.283620	0.185180	-1.532	0.125
For SEX slope, B1				
INTRCPT2, G10	0.446546	0.066993	6.666	0.000
For PPED slope, B2				
INTRCPT2, G20	-0.536378	0.088479	-6.062	0.000

```
The outcome variable is      REP1

Final estimation of fixed effects
(Population-average model with robust standard errors)
```

Fixed Effect	Coefficient	Standard Error	T-ratio	P-value
For INTRCPT1, B0				
INTRCPT2, G00	-1.748402	0.082158	-21.281	0.000
MSESC, G01	-0.283620	0.196005	-1.447	0.148
For SEX slope, B1				
INTRCPT2, G10	0.446546	0.062788	7.112	0.000
For PPED slope, B2				
INTRCPT2, G20	-0.536378	0.082221	-6.524	0.000

Batch execution

The interactive session above produced the following newcmd.hlm.

```
#WHLM CMD FILE FOR THAIGRP.SSM
level1:REP1=INTRCPT1+SEX+PPED+random
level2:INTRCPT1=INTRCPT2+MSESC,2+random/
level2:SEX=INTRCPT2/
level2:PPED=INTRCPT2/
nonlin:binomial,TRIAL
microit:20
```

```
stopmicro:0.000010
macroit:25
stopmacro:0.000100
fixsigma2:1.000000
levlols:10
fixtau:3
accel:5
resfil:n
hypoth:n
CONSTRAIN:n
title:Binomial analysis, Thailand data
output:thaibnml.lis
```

The only important difference between this command file and the command file for Case 1 is the line

```
nonlin:binomial,TRIAL
```

which indicates the type of model and the variable indicating the number of trials. If the user wished to estimate a model with overdispersion in the batch mode, the line

```
fixsigma2:1.000000
```

would be deleted.

Case 3: Poisson model with equal exposure

Suppose that the outcome variable in Case 1 had been the number of days absent during the previous year rather than grade repetition. This outcome would be a non-negative integer, that is, a count rather than a dichotomy. Thus, the Poisson model with a log link would be a reasonable choice for the model. Notice that the time interval during which the absences could accumulate, that is, one year, would be the same for each student. We call this a case of "equal exposure," meaning that each level-1 case had an "equal opportunity" to accumulate absences. (Case 4 describes an example where exposure varies across level-1 cases.)

This model has exactly the same logic as in Case 1 except that the type of model and therefore the corresponding link function will be different. The model choice would be as follows:

```
Do you want to do a nonlinear analysis?  Y

Enter type of nonlinear analysis:

     1) Bernoulli (0 or 1)
     2) Binomial (count)
     3) Poisson  (constant exposure)
     4) Poisson  (variable exposure)

type of analysis:  3
```

Using the batch mode, the model choice would be indicated as

```
NONLIN:POISSON
```

The HLM output would describe the model as follows:

```
Level-1 Model

    E(Y|B) = L
    V(Y|B) = L
```

This is the program's way of saying that the level-1 sampling model is Poisson with equal exposure per level-1 case. The above equation, written with subscripts and Greek letters, is

$$E(Y_{ij}|\beta_j) = \lambda_{ij}$$
$$Var(Y_{ij}|\beta_j) = \lambda_{ij} ,$$

where λ_{ij} ij is the "true" rate of absence for child ij.

```
    log(L) = B0 + B1*(SEX) + B2*(PPED)
```

Notice that the log link replaces the logit link when we have count data. In the example above, β_2 is the expected difference in log-absenteeism between two children of the same sex attending the same school. To translate back to the rate of absenteeism, we would expect a child with pre-primary experience to have $\exp\{\beta_2\}$ times the absenteeism rate of a child attending the same school who did not have pre-primary experience (holding sex constant). In this particular case, the estimated effect for β_2 is most plausibly negative; their $\exp\{\beta_2\}$ is less than 1.0 so that pre-primary experience would reduce the rate of absenteeism.

```
    B0 = G00 + G01*(MSESC) + U0
    B1 = G10
    B2 = G20
```

Notice that the level-2 structural models are identical to those in Case 1.

```
Level-1 variance = 1/L
```

In the metric of the linearized dependent variable, the level-1 variance is the reciprocal of the Poisson variance, λ_{ij}.

Case 4: Poisson model with variable exposure

Suppose that the frequency of a given kind of cancer were tabulated for each of many counties. For example, with five age-groups, the data could be organized so that each county had five counts, with Y_{ij} being the number of cancers in age-group i of county j and n_{ij} being the population size of that age group in that county. A Poisson model with variable exposure would be appropriate, n_{ij} is the variable measuring exposure.

Thus, the model choice would be as follows in the interactive session:

```
Do you want to do a nonlinear analysis? Y

Enter type of nonlinear analysis:

    1) Bernoulli (0 or 1)
    2) Binomial (count)
    3) Poisson  (constant exposure)
    4) Poisson  (variable exposure)

type of analysis: 4
```

After specification of the level-1 variables, the prompt will appear:

```
For the nonlinear analysis, which variable indicates the exposure?
```

The user will choose the exposure variable from the given list.

Using the batch mode, the model choice would be indicated as

```
NONLIN:POISSON,SIZE
```

if *SIZE* is the population size, n_{ij}, for age-group i in county j.

The HLM output would describe the model as follows:

```
Level-1 Model

    E(Y|B) = SIZE*L
    V(Y|B) = SIZE*L
```

This is the program's way of saying that the level-1 sampling model is Poisson equal exposure per level-1 case, so that the above equation, written with subscripts and Greek letters, is

$$E(Y_{ij}|\boldsymbol{\beta}_j) = n_{ij} * \lambda_{ij}$$
$$Var(Y_{ij}|\boldsymbol{\beta}_j) = n_{ij} * \lambda_{ij} ,$$

where λ_{ij} is the "true" cancer rate for age-group i in county j.

```
    log(L) = B0 + B1*(SEX) + B2*(PPED)
```

Notice that the log link replaces the logit link when we have count data.

```
Level-2 Model

    B0 = G00 + G01*(MSESC) + U0
    B1 = G10
    B2 = G20
```

Notice that the level-2 structural models are identical to those in Case 1.

```
Level-1 variance = 1/(Size*L)
```

In the metric of the linearized dependent variable, the level-1 variance is the reciprocal of the Poisson variance, $n_{ij}\lambda_{ij}$.

Fitting HGLMs with three levels

For simplicity of exposition, all of the examples above have used the two-level HGLM. These procedures generalize directly to three-level applications. Again the user must specify the type of nonlinear model desired at level-1. There are now, however, structural models at both levels 2 and 3 as in the case of HLM/3L. Any user familiar with HLM/3L will find the extension to nonlinear analyses straightforward.

7 Plausible Value Averaging with HLM/2L

Version 4 of HLM enables users to produce correct HLM estimates when using datasets that contain two or more plausible values. One such dataset is the National Assessment of Educational progress (NAEP), a U.S. Department of Education achievement test given to a national sample of fourth, eighth, and twelfth graders. HLM makes the applications to datasets such as NAEP accessible to more researchers. It ensures that users new to plausible values and/or HLM will be able to use such datasets as NAEP accurately.

Special procedures and calculations are necessary when estimating any statistical parameters and their standard errors with datasets such as NAEP, due to the use of balanced incomplete block (BIB) spiraling in the administration of the NAEP assessment battery. Every student was not tested on the same items, so item response theory (IRT) was used to estimate proficiency scores for each individual student. This procedure estimated a range or distribution of plausible values for each student's proficiency rather than an individual, observed score. NAEP drew five plausible values at random from the conditional distribution of proficiency scores for each student. The measurement error is due to the fact that these scores are estimated, rather than observed.

In general, these plausible values are used to produce parameter estimates in the following way.

- ❑ Each parameter is estimated for each of the five plausible values, and the five estimates are averaged.
- ❑ Then, the standard error for this average estimate is calculated using the approach recommended by Little & Schenker (1995).

This formula essentially combines the average of the sampling error from the five estimates with the variance between the five estimates multiplied with a factor related to the number of plausible values. This latter value is the measurement error.

In an HLM analysis, the parameter estimates are based on the average parameter estimates from separate HLM analyses of five plausible values. That is, a separate HLM analysis is conducted on each of the five plausible values. The results from the five analyses are averaged, and the standard errors are calculated as outlined above.

Without HLM version 4, these procedures could be performed by producing HLM estimates for each plausible value, and then averaging the estimates and calculating the standard errors using another computer program. These procedures are tedious and time-consuming, especially when performed on many models, grades, and dependent variables.

HLM version 4 takes the plausible values into account in generating the HLM estimates. For each HLM model, the program runs each of the five (or the number specified) plausible values internally, and produces their average value and the correct standard errors. The user seems to be producing one estimate, but the five HLM estimates from the five plausible values are produced and their average and measurement error calculated correctly, thus ensuring an accurate treatment of plausible value data. The output is similar to the standard HLM program output, except that all the components are averaged over estimates derived from the five plausible values. In addition, the output from the five plausible value runs is available in a separate output file.

Calculations performed

The program conducts a separate HLM analysis for each plausible value. The output of the separate HLM analyses is written to files with consecutive numbers, for example, OUT.1, OUT.2, OUT.3, etc. Then, HLM calculates the average of the parameter estimates from the separate analyses and computes the standard errors. The output of the average HLM parameter estimates and their standard errors is found in the output file with the extension AVG.

Averaged parameter estimates   The following parameter estimates are averaged by HLM:

- ❏ The gammas
- ❏ The reliabilities
- ❏ The parameter variances (tau) and its correlations
- ❏ The chi-square values to test whether the parameter variance is zero
- ❏ The standard errors for the variance-covariance components (full maximum likelihood estimates)
- ❏ Multivariate hypothesis testing for fixed effects

Standard error of the gammas   The standard error of the averaged gammas is estimated as described below. The Student's t-value is calculated by dividing the average gamma by its standard error, and the probability of the t-value is estimated from a standard t-distribution table.

The standard error of the gammas consists of two components — sampling error and measurement error. The following routine provided in the NAEP *Data Files User Guide* (Rogers, *et al.*, 1992) is used to approximate the component of error variance due to the error in measurement and to add it to the sampling error.

Let $\hat{\theta}_m$ ($m = 1, \ldots, M$) represent the m-th plausible value. Let $\hat{t}_m$ represent the parameter estimate based on the m-th plausible value. Let U_m represent the variance of $\hat{t}_m$, or the sampling error.

- ❏ Five HLM runs were conducted based on each plausible value $\hat{\theta}_m$. The parameter estimates from these runs were averaged:

$$t^* = \frac{\sum_{m=1}^{M} \hat{t}_m}{M}$$

- ❏ The variance of the parameters from these runs were averaged:

$$U^* = \frac{\sum_{m=1}^{M} U_m}{M}$$

- The variance of the m estimates, $\hat{t}_m$, was estimated:

$$B_m = \frac{\sum_{m=1}^{M}(\hat{t}_m - t^*)^2}{(M-1)}$$

- The final estimate of the variance of the parameter estimate is the sum of the two components:

$$V = U^* + (1 + M^{-1})B_m$$

The square root of this variance is the standard error of the gamma, and it is used in a standard Student's t formula to evaluate the statistical significance of each gamma.

Working with plausible values in HLM

The plausible value feature of HLM/2L must be invoked in Windows or batch mode; there is no interactive mode implemented. To run a plausible value analysis in the batch mode, specify the following line in the command file:

plausvals:*varlist*

Replace *varlist* with the names of the multiple plausible values, separated by commas. The first plausible value must also be specified in the level-1 equation. That plausible value variable may be either a dependent or independent variable, but only *one* such variable may be specified per analysis. Currently, plausible-value analysis is available only for 2-level models.

Example Five plausible values are used, *pvcomp1* through *pvcomp5*. The first one is specified on the level1 line as the dependent variable and also appears as the first element on the plausvals line. The remaining four plausible values follow.

```
level1:PVCOMP1=intrcpt1+ses+random
level2:intrcpt1=intrcpt2+school+random/
level2:ses=intrcpt2+school+random/
plausvals:PVCOMP1,PVCOMP2,PVCOMP3,PVCOMP4,PVCOMP5
```

The output contains averaged results of T, correlations and reliabilities of T, σ^2, the gamma table (with averaged standard errors), a χ^2 table, and, if requested, the general linear hypothesis tables. All other output options may be present in the output for the separate runs, but not in the averaged output.

References

Barnett, Marshall, Raudenbush, & Brennan (1993)
Gender and the relationship between job experiences and psychological distress: a study of dual-earner couples.
Journal of Personality and Social Psychology, **64**, 794–806.

Breslow, N. & Clayton, D.G. (1993)
Approximate inference in generalized linear mixed models.
Journal of the American Statistical Association, **88**, 9–25.

Goldstein, H. (1991)
Nonlinear multilevel models with an application to discrete response data.
Biometrika, **78**, 45–51.

Hedeker, D., & Gibbons, R. (1994)
A random-effects ordinal regression model for multilevel analysis.
Biometrics, **50**, 933–44.

Little, R., & Schenker, N. (1995)
Missing data.
In: Arminger, G., Clogg, C.C., & Sobel, M.E.: *Handbook of Statistical Modeling for the Social and Behavioral Sciences*.
New York: Plenum Press.

Longford, N. (1993)
Random Coefficient Models.
Oxford: Clarendon Press.

McCullagh, P., & Nelder, J. (1989)
Generalized Linear Models, 2nd Edition.
London: Chapman and Hill.

Raudenbush, S.W., & Bryk, A.S. (1987)
Examining correlates of diversity.
Journal of Educational Statistics, **12**, 241–269.

Raudenbush, S.W., & Bhumirat, C. (1992)
The distribution of resources for primary education and its conse-
quences for teaching and learning in Thailand.
International Journal of Education Research, **17(2)**, 143–164.

Rodriguez, G., & Goldman, N. (1995)
An assessment of estimation procedures for multilevel models with bi-
nary responses.
Journal of the Royal Statistical Society, Series A, **158**, 73–89.

Rogers, A., *et al.* (1992)
*National Assessment of Educational Progress: 1990 Secondary-use
Data Files User Guide*
Princeton, New Jersey: Educational Testing Service.

Schall, R. (1991)
Estimation in generalized linear models with random effects.
Biometrika, **40**, 719–727.

Stiratelli, R., Laird, N., & Ware, J. (1984)
Random effects models for serial observations with binary response.
Biometrics, **40**, 961–971.

Wong, G., & Mason, W. (1985)
The hierarchical logistic regression model for multilevel analysis.
Journal of the American Statistical Association, **80**(391), 513–524.

Yang, M. (1995)

A simulation study for the assessment of the non-linear hierarchical model estimation via approximate maximum likelihood.

Unpublished apprenticeship paper, College of Education, Michigan State University.

Zeger, S., Liang, K., & Albert, P. (1988)

Models for longitudinal data: A likelihood approach.

Biometrics, **44**, 1049–1060.

Author Index

Subject Index

Log link, 151
Logit link, 120, 140
    function, 121

Macro iteration, 124
Mahalanobis distance, 12, 34, 99
Marginalized quasi-likelihood,
    128
Maximum-likelihood
    estimate, 5, 81
Meta-analysis, example, 71
Micro iteration, 124
Missing data, 10, 87
Model checking, 11, 32, 99
Model specification, 11, 90,
    107, 133
MQL, 128
Multiple constraints, 63
Multivariate tests, 56

NAEP, 155
Nested model, 82
Nested structure, 1
No-intercept model, 60
nobase keyword, 60
nonlin keyword, 48
Nonlinear analysis, 133
numit keyword, 47

OL estimate, 12, 47
OL prefix, 6
OL residual, 32, 37
Oneway ANOVA, 48
Option, 40, 103
output keyword, 48

Pairwise deletion, 10
Parameter estimation, 4, 81
Penalized quasi-likelihood, 123
Plausible value, 155
plausvals keyword, 158
Poisson
    example, 150, 152
    model, 126, 127
Population-average model, 128,
    130
PQL, 123
    full, 131
    restricted, 131
Properties of the estimators, 128
PRSSM2 program, 10
PRSSM3 program, 84

Quasi-likelihood
    estimation, 131
    marginalized, 128
    penalized, 123

Random Coefficient Model, 49
Regression with Means as
    Outcomes, 49
Reliability, 52, 81
RELIABILITY ESTIMATES, 5
Reliability of $\hat{\beta}_{qj}$, 5
resfil keyword, 32, 48
Residual analysis, 35
Residual file, 11, 12, 32, 33, 34,
    99
Restricted maximum likelihood,
    82
Restricted PQL, 131
RSP file, 19, 102

Sampling schemes, 67
SAS file, 13, 89
SAS V5 transport file, 13
Shrunken estimate, 4
SIGMA-SQUARED, 5
SSM file, 9, 10, 11, 19, 84, 102,
      133
   example, 88
STS file, 19
SYSTAT
   file, 13, 19, 89
   input, 19

TAU, 5
Tau (T), dispersion matrix, 3, 79
Tau (beta), 80, 81
Tau (pi), 79, 80
teacher.dat, 71
teacher.lis, 73
teacher.rsp, 72
thaibern.lis, 137, 138
thaibnml.lis, 146
thaigrp.hlm, 149
Thailand data, 134
thaiugrp.hlm, 143
Three-level HGLM, 154
Three-level model, 77, 78
title keyword, 48

Unit-specific model, 128, 130

V-known program, 35, 70, 73
Vocabulary growth study, 61

Weighting, 66, 69
   example, 68, 70